The C of a Child

LIVING STANDARDS FOR THE 1990s

Nina Oldfield and Autumn C S Yu

CPAG Ltd, 1-5 Bath Street, London EC1V 9PY

CPAG promotes action for the relief, directly or indirectly, of poverty among children and families with children. We work to ensure that those on low incomes get their full entitlements to welfare benefits. In our campaigning and information work we seek to improve benefits and policies for low income families, in order to eradicate the injustice of poverty. If you are not already supporting us, please consider a donation, or ask for details of our membership schemes and publications.

Child Poverty Action Group, 1-5 Bath Street, London EC1V 9PY

© CPAG Ltd, 1993

ISBN 0 946744 56 4

Poverty Publication 85

A CIP record for this book is available from the British Library

Cover and design: Devious Designs, Sheffield S2 2SF
Cover photograph: Sally and Richard Greenhill, London N1 1NL
Typesetting: Nancy White, London N1 1EA
Printing: Calvert's Press, London E2 7DJ

CONTENTS

ACKNOWLEDGEMENTS

This book produces an estimate of how much it costs to maintain children of different ages and sex in the family in Britain today.

It draws on the work of the Family Budget Unit, a group of social scientists and those interested in the domestic economy, who came together in 1985. Funded by the Joseph Rowntree Foundation research was undertaken on the origins, methods and use of budget standards in different countries.[1] This led to a two-year project, again funded by the Joseph Rowntree Foundation, designed to produce budget standards for six model families. The research project involved three centres. The food budget was drawn up by nutritionists Dr Michael Nelson, Anne-Marie Mayer and Penny Manley at the Department of Nutrition and Dietetics, King's College, University of London. The leisure, household goods and services budget and clothing budgets were drawn up by home economists based at the Department of Leisure and Food Management at Sheffield City Polytechnic including Mary McCabe, Audrey Rose, Alan Waddington and Professor David Kirk (now at the Department of Hospitality Studies, Queen Margaret College, Edinburgh). The fuel budget was prepared by Sandra Hutton and Bill Wilkinson in the Social Policy Research Unit at the University of York. The overall project was coordinated at first by Dr John Ernst and then by Dr Leslie Hicks in the Department of Social Policy and Social Work at the University of York and they also prepared the housing and transport budgets. Professor Jonathan Bradshaw directed the whole project.[2]

The research was overseen by an advisory committee who in addition to the principal researchers included Dr Janet Lewis, Anne Muir, Freda Patton and Hermione Parker, who was also responsible for editing the working papers arising out of the work. Those responsible for drawing up the budgets for each commodity were supported by expert groups, specialists in the subject matter.

We also wish to thank all those who were involved – in particular the Joseph Rowntree Foundation and the ESRC for their financial support, and Paul Stanley for his contributions to the low cost budget and his proofreading of the final manuscript. We are grateful for having had the opportunity to contribute to the work of the Family Budget Unit as doctoral students in the Department of Social Policy and Social Work at the University of York. We and not the Family Budget Unit are responsible for any faults in the analysis outlined in this book.

Finally, thanks are also due to Carey Oppenheim, Sally Witcher and Saul Becker for their valuable comments on the manuscript, Debbie Licorish for editorial and production work, Nigel Taylor for his text and cover design, Nancy White and Calvert's Press for producing the book, and to Peter Ridpath for his promotion work.

NOTES

1   J Bradshaw, D Mitchell and J Morgan, 'Evaluating Adequacy: The potential of budget standards', *Journal of Social Policy* 16:2, pp165-81, 1987

2   The results of the work of the Family Budget Unit are presented in more detail in J Bradshaw, *Budget Standards for the United Kingdom*, Avebury (forthcoming), and more briefly in J Bradshaw, *Household Budgets and Living Standards*, a Joseph Rowntree Report, 1993

PREFACE

State Parties recognise the right of every child to a standard of living adequate for the child's physical, mental, spiritual, moral and social development.

Article 27 United Nations Convention on the Rights of a Child

Parents, families, the community and society as a whole can provide the kind of standard of living for children envisaged in the UN Convention on the Rights of a Child, to which the UK government is a signatory. And yet the research we are publishing here adds to the growing evidence that income support – the key social security benefit and the safety net below which no one should fall – is failing to provide for the most minimal needs of children.

The 'cost of a child' has always been a central concern of the Child Poverty Action Group, not surprisingly, given our name. The question of how to measure a child's cost and by whom and how it should be met has been hotly debated for many years. But the issue has gained new importance for three main reasons: the very high instances of child poverty in the UK, the heated debates about the future of family policy and the controversial arguments about the future of social security.

Firstly, children are at greater risk of poverty than the rest of society. The latest government figures, *Households below Average Income*, reveal that in 1990/91 nearly a third of all children in the UK (3.9 million) were living in poverty – ie, on incomes below half the average after housing costs (compared to a quarter of society as a whole).[1] In 1979 there were 1.4 million children (10%) in the same position. Other data show that 2.7 million, well over one-fifth of all children in Britain, were living on income support in 1992.[2]

Secondly, the future of the family has stormed on to the political agenda once again. There are strong differences of view within the political parties and society as a whole about the rapidity of the social and demographic changes that have dramatically altered our notions of the 'family'. Lone parents, as usual, have borne the brunt of the glare of publicity – some informed, much of it not. But amid this debate the child and his or her future is often buried. The children of lone parents are particularly at risk of poverty, largely because the majority of lone parents are trapped on benefits. In 1991-2, 72% of lone parents lived on income support – two-fifths of them for three years and more, and many of them for much longer than three years. The government's principal response to lone parents and their children's poverty has been the Child Support Act, implemented in April 1993. This Act aims to enforce the payment of maintenance from the absent parent. Although the CSA is not the subject of this book, as explained by Jonathan Bradshaw in the pages which follow, the maintenance payable for the children is based on the income support child allowances and yet there has been no proper assessment of the adequacy of those allowances.

Thirdly, social security is rarely out of the headlines as the major political parties review their policies and spending root and branch. Within this broad debate children and how we should support them are a central issue. In particular, child benefit's future as a universal benefit has been questioned yet again.

It is in this context that we are publishing *The Cost of a Child*. This research has been conducted by the Family Budget Unit (FBU) at the University of York. The findings contained here provide a crucial contribution to assessing the adequacy of social security benefits. It is important to stress just how rarely such an exercise has been undertaken – income support is the newest version of national assistance established in 1948 as a result of the Beveridge Report.[3] Since that date, the scales which were set then have never been reassessed in a systematic way. Thus one in six of the population are reliant on a benefit that is paid without any examination of how far it can meet people's basic needs. In fact, there has been mounting evidence of the inadequacy of income support. The work we publish here adds further to this evidence.

Children's costs can be looked at in a number of different ways. There are direct costs, which are in a sense the most obvious – for example, food, clothing, toys, heating and so on. There are also indirect costs. These include opportunity costs and the costs of unpaid labour. Heather Joshi has estimated that a woman on average earnings may forgo £202,500 in lost earnings over her lifetime as a result of having two children.[4] (This assumes that she spends eight years out of the labour market and returns to work part-time on lower earnings.) David Piachaud, in a study for CPAG, estimated that women undertook 44 hours a week child care out of 50 in total and that this work contributed around 6% to the Gross National Product.[5]

This research is about the direct costs of children, and resurrects an old method used in social science known as the budget standard. This was adopted by Rowntree in his seminal work on poverty. It is still used widely in other countries. A 'budget standard' is a specified basket of goods and services which when priced represents a standard of living. The researchers choose two standards of living by estimating a **modest-but-adequate budget** and a **low cost budget**. The items and services which are included in each of these budgets are chosen by a group of experts and are also informed by what people actually spend their money on. In addition, the low cost budget is informed by the *Breadline Britain* survey which determined what people thought were necessities.

The detailed research findings contained in the pages which follow describe the assumptions and methods they use at some length. Below we summarise the key results. In April 1993, using a **modest-but-adequate budget**:

- The weekly cost of a child aged 4 was around £62, it fell to around £56 for a child aged 10 and rose again to £65 for a child aged 16.
- For pre-school children the largest cost was child care, making up around 30% of the total cost.
- Major costs were food, clothing and housing.
- Excluding child care costs, the cost of a child increased with age.
- Boys cost more than girls.
- There was no difference in the costs according to tenure in 1993. However, in 1991, when the research was first conducted and house prices were higher, the cost of a child in an owner occupied home was higher due to her/his share of the mortgage.
- A one child family is more expensive than a two child family because there are no economies of scale, in particular in relation to housing costs and baby sitting costs. The extra costs of a one child family amount to between £7 and £8 a week.

Using the **low cost budget** in April 1993:

- The cost of a child under 11 was £30.37 a week and £41.71 for a child aged 16.
- Food made up the largest component of the cost of the child aged under 11 years, accounting for a third of the cost.
- A low cost budget for a family with two children was 30% higher than the rate of income support.
- A family with two children would have needed an extra £34 a week above IS to achieve a low cost budget and a lone parent with two children would have needed an extra £23 a week.

- Child benefit met only 35% of the cost of a child in a two child family (a shortfall of £16.57), income support child allowance met only 59% (a shortfall of £10.57) and the income support child allowance in addition to the family premium met only 78% (a shortfall of £5.74).
- Fuel costs in the low cost budget were higher than in the modest-but-adequate budget because poorer families tend to have homes which are more difficult to heat and they heat their homes for longer periods as they are likely to spend more time there.

Behind the bare statistics lie important findings which can and should inform current debates. Child care emerges as a major cost in the modest-but-adequate budget of a pre-school child and yet the UK has the lowest level of subsidised child care in the European Community after Portugal.[6] The dramatic case, recently reported in the press, of a woman jailed for six months for leaving her two-year-old daughter alone in her home while she worked, because she could not afford child care, is a tragic reminder of the high costs and choices people face.[7] Improving child care provision could be a crucial tool in enabling lone parents to enter the labour market and reduce their reliance on social security. The necessities of life – food, clothing, heating and housing – account for large chunks of both budgets. In the case of food, a third of a low cost budget for a child goes on food. This is important evidence in the debate about extending VAT to items which are currently zero-rated – such as food and children's clothing and, until 1994, fuel. As the FBU research shows, fuel costs are higher in a low cost budget than a modest-but-adequate budget – thus poorer families are likely to have higher fuel costs and will be harder hit by the imposition of VAT on domestic fuel. If VAT were extended to other basic items it would have a devastating impact on the living standards of children in low income families. But above all the research shows that the levels of income support for children are far below the most minimum of needs in today's society.

The research also opens up the important debate of what constitutes an *adequate* standard of living for children. The low cost budget includes some leisure items and services. Thus it is making an important statement about the fact that children on low incomes should have access not only to food, clothing and shelter, but also to the educational and social goods that ensure that children can develop their potential in these areas.

The task of deciding how the costs of children are borne lies beyond the scope of this paper. CPAG has argued that it is society's responsiblity to meet the basic costs of children just as it meets the educational and health needs of children. What is clear is that well over a fifth of children in Britain are living on benefits which cannot provide them with a standard of living to enable them to develop physically, emotionally and socially. It is essential that we address the causes and consequences of such policies, not only for children's futures but also for society as a whole.

Carey Oppenheim
Research and Information Officer
Child Poverty Action Group

NOTES

1   Department of Social Security, *Households below Average Income, A Statistical Analysis 1979-1990/91*, HMSO, 1993
2   Department of Social Security Press Release, *Income Support – 1992 Annual Statistical Enquiry*, 24 May 1993
3   Sir William Beveridge, *Social Insurance and Allied Services*, Cmnd 6404, 1942
4   H Joshi, 'The Cost of Caring', in C Glendinning and J Miller (eds), *Women and Poverty in Britain, the 1990s*, Wheatsheaf, 1992
5   D Piachaud, *Round about 50 Hours a Week*, CPAG Ltd, 1984
6   P Moss, *Childcare and Equality of Opportunity*, Commission of the European Communities, 1988
7   *The Guardian*, 3 August 1993

FOREWORD

In 1979 the Child Poverty Action Group published David Piachaud's *The Cost of a Child*. That seminal study and Margaret Wynn's important book on family policy[1] influenced the establishment of the Family Budget Unit on whose work this book is based. Although this book presents what I believe is the most elaborate and careful attempt to establish the cost of a child it is only one attempt, using only one of the available methods.

Discovering the cost of a child is an important endeavour for social scientists. Every welfare state in the industrial world has developed a package of benefits and services that assist parents in the important task of raising the next generation of children. The degree to which that package meets that task is a measure of the commitment of the state to families bearing the costs of child-rearing. We need to know what proportion of the costs of a child is covered by child benefit, the most important element of the package in the United Kingdom. This is estimated here. Attempting to establish the cost of a child also makes it possible to evaluate the adequacy of boarding out allowances paid by local authorities to foster carers. This is also estimated here. Discovering the cost has also been given a new importance by the establishment of the Child Support Agency. The calculation of maintenance requirements is intended to represent the day-to-day cost of looking after a child based on the prevailing income support allowances.

So we come to the issue which is of greatest relevance to CPAG: what does this research tell us about the adequacy of the scales of benefit paid to families on income support? One in six people in Britain are now dependent for whole or part of their incomes on income support and many others are living below or only a little above that benefit.[2] There are 2.7 million children living in families receiving income support and the number has doubled since 1979. Although there may have been a small increase in the real level of the income support scales (depending on the level of water rates and take up of the social fund), the standard of living of families with children on income support has fallen since 1979 in comparison with that of the working population. Furthermore, there is now considerable evidence[3] that families with children living on income support are particularly hard-pressed. The income support scales are derived from the Rowntree's work[4] using budget standards and, since 1948, have been uprated on the basis of historical precedent, opportunism and political hunch. They have never been systematically reassessed. It is hard to bring to life the lifestyles of the very large number of families living on these benefits so that a judgement can be made about the adequacy of the scales in the context of the modern standards of living in Britain.

In this book we have derived a low cost budget for a child. We have found that it is higher than the income support scales for children. Unlike child benefit, the child rates of income support are designed to meet all the needs of a child. So either our low cost standard is too high or the income support scales for children are too low...

The purpose of this kind of analysis is to convey to us all, and particularly to those who are making judgements about the level of benefits paid to families with children, the reality of the living standards and consumption patterns on income support.

In making judgements, be aware that between 1979 and 1991 average living standards increased by over 30%. However, inequalities widened dramatically, families with children drifted down the income distribution scale and many more families found themselves dependent on income support and relatively worse off. This need not have happened. It was the result of this government's tax, benefit and employment policies. If we are to begin to improve the living standards of children and avoid separating the very large number of them on income support from normal patterns of life in Britain, then the child scale rates of income support must be increased now.

Professor Jonathan Bradshaw
University of York
July 1993

NOTES

1   M Wynn, *Family Policy: A study of the economic costs of rearing children and their social and political consequences*, Michael Joseph, 1972

2   Social Security Committee, *Low Income Statistics: Low Income Families 1979-1989*, 2nd Report, HMSO, 1992

3   J Millar, *Poverty and the Lone Parent Family*, Avebury: Gower, 1989; J Bradshaw and H Holmes, *Living on the Edge: A Study of the Living Standards of Families on Benefit in Tyne and Wear*, CPAG Ltd, 1989; J Bradshaw and J Morgan, *Budgeting*

on Benefit: The consumption of families on social security, Family Policy Studies Centre, 1987

4   See F Field, *What Price a Child? A historical review of the relative cost of dependants*, Studies of the Social Security System No 8, Policy Studies Institute, 1985; J Bradshaw, 'Welfare benefits' in R Walker and G Parker (eds), *Money Matters, Income, Wealth and Financial Welfare*, Sage, 1988

Introduction

There are two kinds of costs which have dominated the contemporary debate on the financial cost of child rearing:

- **Direct costs**, which are the actual costs of children's clothing, and leisure, and food and so on. A valuable contribution to this approach was made by Piachaud's studies of child costs.[1]
- **Indirect costs**, which are the opportunity costs of child rearing such as the lost earnings of parents. Joshi calculated the earnings lost by mothers in all phases of employment and potential employment as a result of child rearing.[2] Other studies have investigated additional elements of indirect cost – for example, Piachaud estimated the hours spent by parents caring for children under five.[3] This highlighted non-market as well as market costs in parenting, such as loss of sleep or personal leisure time.

The focus of this study is the direct costs of a child.

STUDIES OF THE COST OF A CHILD

A number of different approaches have been used to estimate the cost of a child.

THE LARGE SURVEY APPROACH

This is based on large surveys on what families actually spend, such as the *Family Expenditure Survey*.[4] In this approach the cost of children can be estimated by comparing the expenditure of families with children to those without children to determine the child's share of family expenditure. Moreover, economists use complex equations for the construction of equivalence scales based on similar household consumption data to estimate the proportion of household cost that can be attributed to children. These scales are used to adjust the income need of families to take account of their child's age, and family size.[5] There is some controversy about which of a number of scales best describes the cost of a child in relation to family costs.[6]

THE CONSENSUAL APPROACH

This involves asking individuals what they think they need to spend on selected budget items or services. Piachaud's survey of teenagers employed this method as a base for estimates of older child costs.[7]

THE BUDGET STANDARD APPROACH

This estimates what families *ought* to spend rather than what they actually *do* (or think they need to) spend on childrearing. A characteristic of this approach is that normative judgement is used to create a basket of goods and services which represents the type of commodities, quantities and quality of family consumption.[8]

Budget standards are among the oldest methodological tools in the social sciences. The method was pioneered by Rowntree at the beginning of this century and informed Beveridge's recommendations for the setting of the National Assistance scales (the predecessor to supplementary benefit and income support). Since the war the method has been little used in the UK, with the exception of Piachaud's study in the late 1970s. Outside the UK, budget standards research has not been as neglected. In the United States, the Bureau of Labor Statistics published regular updated budget standards from 1946–80, and such standards are still produced regularly in some states. Canada, Sweden, Norway and Holland use budget standards, and Denmark is at present setting up a budget standard programme. In Britain in 1985 a group of social scientists set up the Family Budget Unit (FBU) to produce budgets for a number of model family types.

The method used in this study follows the budget standard approach.

THE FAMILY BUDGET MODEL

The process of arriving at the cost of a child in this study involves establishing a family budget for a number of family types from which the child's share is determined. The task of those who are drawing up a budget is to decide what *items* are included in the budget, what *quantity* of items are included, what *quality* the item should have, what *price* should be given to it and, where the item is purchased intermittently or occasionally, what *lifetime* should be attributed to it – ie, how long it should last. The approach to carrying out these tasks varies between commodities in the budget but in general the following methods have been used.

- Those responsible for preparing the budget for each commodity have been supported by groups of experts. These groups have been made up of specialists in the commodity. Thus the fuel group consisted of experts on domestic energy consumption including representatives of the fuel industries. The food group comprised nutritionists and experts on food consumption.
- This expert advice has been supplemented by seeking, where it is available, behavioural information about what people actually do. So the *National Food Survey*[9] helped to inform the food budget. The *National Travel Survey*[10] was drawn on for the travel budget. The FBU have sought out and collected market research reports on consumption patterns, and made heavy use of the *General Household Survey*.[11]
- The budget has also been informed by recommended standards – ie, standards which have been laid down by official bodies. So, for example, the housing budget has been drawn up with regard to fitness standards and common bedroom standards; the food budget takes account of the NACNE[12] guidelines on recommended dietary amounts; and the BREDEM (Building Research Establishment Domestic Energy Model)[13] has been used to determine the fuel needed for the particular homes specified in the study.
- Previous budget standards have been drawn on. Other people in other countries have gone through these tasks before and so, where no authoritative information in Britain was found, other people's standards have been drawn on, in particular the Swedish,[14] Canadian[15] and Norwegian[16] budgets.
- In the end, the FBU have used their own judgements about what is right and what is appropriate, sometimes overriding expert opinion or behavioural evidence.
- A second stage has validated what has gone into the budget by comparing

the budgets drawn up with actual expenditure patterns based on the annual *Family Expenditure Survey*.[17] The FBU have been careful not to use the FES to *determine* the budgets, because of the desire to separate themselves from what people's behaviour is – the essence of budget standards is to draw up what is fundamentally a normative budget, unconstrained by income or taste.

• As well as returning to the groups of experts, groups of consumers have looked at the budgets. They have been asked to comment on the details and the budgets have been adjusted in the light of the feedback from this exercise.

The balance between the different methods, and decisions about which one has authority over another, was determined pragmatically. There was no set order. It depended on the information and evidence available and which commodity was being considered.

The initial budget sought to represent a modest-but-adequate standard of living, not a poverty or minimum standard. This distinguished the research from the earlier approaches which follow a tradition of minimum subsistence budgets. The modest-but-adequate standard was first used in 1948 by the United States Bureau of Labor Statistics in its City Worker's Family Budget. It was described as a level of living which is sufficient to 'satisfy prevailing standards of what is necessary for health, efficiency, the nurture of children and for participation in community activities'.[18] A similar concept has been used in budget standards produced in Toronto, Montreal, Norway and Sweden, and reflects the notion of the 'Prevailing Family Standard' defined by the Watts Committee as 'one that affords full opportunity to participate in contemporary society and the basic options it offers. It is moderate in the sense of lying both above the requirements of survival and decency, and well below levels of luxury as generally understood.'[19] Watts used the median expenditure of families with two children to represent this standard.

The model budgets have been drawn up for the following six types of family:

• Single man (aged 30 years)
• Single woman (aged 72 years)
• Two adults (man 34, woman 32)
• Two adults, two children (man 34, woman 32, girl 4, boy 10)
• Two adults, two children (man 37, woman 35, boy 10, girl 16)
• One adult and two children (woman 32, girl 4, boy 10)

These families were selected as representative of major groups in the population, including 'priority groups' such as lone parents, children, and the elderly, and provided a reasonable spread across generations.

A number of other crucial assumptions have to be made about lifestyles, including economic activity, housing tenure and car ownership. These assumptions and the decisions about what is included in the budget are determined as often as not by factual data on what is the most common pattern of behaviour in the community. For the modest-but-adequate budget, a 50% test has been largely applied – if more than 50% of a certain type of family has a certain commodity, then it is assumed that these families have it.

York was selected as the place to price the budget. Rowntree claimed:

> Upon the whole I think it may be said that, viewed from the industrial standpoint, the conditions in York are fairly representative of the average conditions which obtain in other provincial towns.[20]

Whether or not this is still true, the budget needs to be priced in a given place in order to provide it with a local cultural base. As far as possible the budgets were priced using retailers in York with nationwide outlets so the prices do not vary from place to place, although some items may do.[21]

The costs of children are derived from the model family budgets at two standards of living:

- a **modest-but-adequate standard** using the FBU family budgets;
- a **low cost budget** derived by scaling down the modest-but-adequate family budgets.

Chapters 2 and 3 deal with the methods used to derive the modest-but-adequate cost of a child, the costs of a child are summarised commodity by commodity, and the modest-but-adequate costs of children of different ages and sexes, and economies of scale are explored. Chapters 4 and 5 describe and summarise the low cost budget, Chapter 6 compares the two budgets, Chapter 7 compares the modest-but-adequate budget to the level of foster care allowances, and Chapter 8 compares the low cost budget rates with benefit rates.

NOTES

1   D Piachaud, *The Cost of a Child*, CPAG Ltd, 1979, and *Children and Poverty*, CPAG Ltd, 1981

2   H Joshi, *The Cash Opportunity Costs of Childbearing: An Approach to Estimation using British Data*, Paper 208, Centre for Economic Policy Research, 1987

3 D Piachaud, *Round about Fifty Hours a Week: The Time Costs of Children*, CPAG Ltd, 1984

4 The *Family Expenditure Survey* is a government annual survey of the income and expenditure of households in the UK.

5 J Banks and P Johnson, *Children and Household Living Standards*, Institute for Fiscal Studies, 1993; Social Security Select Committee, *Low Income Statistics: Households below Average Income Tables 1988*, First Report 1990-91, House of Commons, 1991; D Conniffe and G Keogh, *Equivalence Scales and Costs of Children*, Paper 142, Economic and Social Research Institute, 1988

6 L D McClements, 'Equivalence Scales for Children', *Journal of Public Economics*, Vol 1, No 2, pp191-210, 1977, and *The Economics of Social Security*, Heinemann, 1978; P Whiteford, *A Family's Needs: Equivalence Scales, Poverty and Social Security*, Research Paper No 27, Development Division, Australian Department of Social Security, 1985

7 D Piachaud, *Children and Poverty*, CPAG Ltd, 1981

8 Child budgets have been created using this process by Piachaud (1979) and K Lovering, *The Cost of Children in Australia*, Working Paper 8, Australian Institute of Family Studies, 1984

9 Ministry of Agriculture, Fisheries and Food, *Household Food Consumption and Expenditure (National Food Survey) 1983-87*, HMSO, 1985-89

10 Department of Transport, *National Travel Survey: 1985-86 Report – Part One, An Analysis of Personal Travel*, HMSO, 1988

11 Office of Population Censuses and Surveys, *General Household Survey 1989*, HMSO, 1991

12 National Advisory Committee on Nutritional Education (NACNE), *Proposals and Guidelines for Health Education in Britain*, Health Education Council, 1983

13 Anderson, et al, *Building Research Establishment Domestic Energy Model (BREDEM): Background, Philosophy and Description*, Building Research Establishment Publications, 1985

14 Swedish National Board for Consumer Policies, *Calculations of Reasonable Costs*, 1989

15 Social Planning Council of Metropolitan Toronto, *The Budgets Guide Methodology Study*, 1981

16 E Borgeraas, *Et Standardbudsjett for Forbruksutgifter*, Statens Institutt for Forbruksforskning, 1987

17 Central Statistical Office, *Family Expenditure Survey 1988*, HMSO, 1989

18 Quoted in M Wynn, *Family Policy: A study of the economic costs of rearing children and their social and political consequences*, Michael Joseph, 1972, p36

19 H Watts, *New American Budget Standards: Report of the Expert Committee on Family Budget Revision*, Institute for Research on Poverty, University of Wisconsin, 1980, pviii

20 B S Rowntree, *Poverty: A Study of Town Life*, Macmillan, 1901, p33

21 The budgets were constructed in two stages. The first stage involved the

formulation of budgets for family types, two adults | (2 adult), two adults and two children aged 4 and 10 (2 adult/2 child), and one adult and two children aged 4 and 10 (1 adult/2 child), at October 1990 prices. After the first stage, there was a period of consultation. Following this, the three other budgets were constructed. With the exception of the food budget, all were priced in October 1991 but have been uprated by the Commodity Retail Price Index (Department of Employment 1993) to April 1993 prices for the purpose of comparing the summary budgets and current benefit rates.

2 The modest-but-adequate standard for a child

The cost of a child can be derived from the family budget standard using what is called either 'deductive' or 'itemised' methods. The deductive method is fairly crude. It provides an estimate of the average cost of children by comparing the difference in costs between the family budget for two parents and two children, and the two adult family budget. The advantages of this method lie in its simple interpretation of costs and its speed of execution. However, it is limited as it fails to distinguish between children of different ages and sexes in families with more than one child, and fails to identify the actual itemised costs. The deductive method was tried and found to produce a lower cost of a child than the itemised method by about 10%.

We prefer to use the itemised estimate of child costs in this study on the grounds that it is a more accurate method. It is used to produce a comprehensive basket of goods and services to meet the needs of boys and girls aged 4, 10 and 16 years of age at a modest-but-adequate standard. Economies of scale are also explored for a first and second child.

A number of processes are used to arrive at the child's itemised budget from the consumption of the family as a whole:

- identifying individual items;
- per capita estimates;
- differential calculations;
- normative judgements on what items can be included relative to children (see below for explanations of these approaches).

THE INDIVIDUAL ITEM APPROACH

This is most commonly used in developing a child's budget standard. It establishes a set of individual child requirements, such as clothing, shoes, etc, leaving adults responsible for their own and shared or fixed household costs. An advantage of using this method alone is that it enables the researcher to set tight parameters around the composition of the child's basket of goods and services; a drawback is the incompleteness of the budget produced.

THE PER CAPITA APPROACH

This is useful for estimating consumption which is shared by all family members and where the distribution of the consumption for individuals in the family is unknown. It provides a simple and effective method of allocating particular expenditure equally to all family members who arguably gain equally from such consumption. Up to a point, the per capita method gives a sliding scale of costs per child as family size increases until the number or size of goods has to be increased. The disadvantage is that, on the whole, it treats children as if they are simply other adults. The result of this generally is to understate the adult proportion of cost and overstate the child's proportion.

THE DIFFERENTIAL CALCULATION

The difference in spending between the couple family and a family with children for similar items of consumption is the extra cost of a child. This extra cost is shared among the children in a family. For example, the child's housing standard is the difference between the cost of a small house suitable for two adults compared to a family-sized house. This approach is useful because it excludes the bulk of the fixed or shared family costs from the child's budget standard. The main disadvantage is that, as the number of items included in the differential calculation increases, the refinement of the calculation decreases. This approach is also only useful where the different family types have similar goods of similar quality.

NORMATIVE JUDGEMENTS

Where responsibility for costs are in doubt, normative judgement is used to establish the inclusion of items in the child's basket of goods, or to set the proportion of costs that should be considered as the extra cost of children.

An advantage of using this technique is the level of detail it achieves. This process allows for higher proportions of cost to be assigned to each child's budget – eg, a higher share of internal decorating costs can be attributed to young children than a simple per capita share. The disadvantage of this approach stems from the length of time needed to develop and update the budgets, and the subjective nature of the decision making.

THE MODEST-BUT-ADEQUATE BUDGET COMPONENTS

The following pages give a brief description of how each component of the child's budget was constructed to represent a modest-but-adequate standard of living. The components are:

- Housing
- Fuel
- Food
- Clothing
- Household goods and services
- Child care
- Transport
- Leisure goods and services
- Personal care
- Pocket money

HOUSING

Providing a roof over a child's head is a major component of a cost of a child. Housing expenditure at the modest-but-adequate standard of living is largely determined by the size of the house, which is influenced by family composition. The size and location of the house also affects levels of spending in other parts of the budget, such as household furnishings, fuel use and transport. We have assumed a number of different scenarios (see tables).

Children's housing costs consist of **direct** costs, such as mortgage repayments or rent, and **indirect** costs, such as contents insurance, water rates and maintenance. Table 2 shows what these costs are. The difference in costs for owner occupation reflects the level of borrowing of the owner occupiers at the different stages of their housing career. In a two child family, the average child in a family with an established mortgage incurs a cost of £8.37 or 11% of their aggregate housing expenditure. A child in rented accommodation, however, has lower actual costs but proportionally greater costs of £5.32 or 12% of the total family housing costs.

TABLE 1: **Housing profiles for two family types, October 1991 prices**

Family type	Tenure	Description
2 adult	Rented[1] local authority	1960s flat, 1 bed, 1 mile city centre rent £18.09 week
	Owner occupied[2] new/establish mortgage	1890s part-modernised brick terrace, 2 beds, less than 1 mile city, £44,000
2 adult/2 child	Rented local authority	1930s modernised brick terrace, 3 beds, ½ mile city, rent £26.30 week
	Owner occupied new/establish mortgage	1980s brick semi-detached, 3 beds, 1 mile from city, £55,000.

The figures also illustrate the importance of economies of scale. In families of different sizes the costs are greatest for a child in one child families and, to extrapolate, 50% less for each child in a two child family and so on, until the point is reached when the house will not be big enough to suit a modest-but-adequate lifestyle.

TABLE 2: **Housing costs per child and by family size, October 1991 prices, £ per week**

	ESTABLISHED MORTGAGE		RENTED	
	2 adult/ 2 child	2 adult/ 1 child	2 adult/ 2 child	2 adult/ 1 child
Mortgage repayment*	6.37	12.74	4.11	8.21
Water rates	0.37	0.74	0.01	0.01
Sewerage rates	0.48	0.95	0.05	0.10
Interior decoration	1.15	1.15	1.15	1.15
Total	**8.37**	**15.58**	**5.32**	**9.47**

* Mortgage repayments per child for new mortgage holders are £12.87 in 2 adult/2 child, and £25.74 in 2 adult/1 child families.

METHODS

DIRECT HOUSING COSTS OF CHILDREN

REPAYMENT MORTGAGE, EXCLUDING MORTGAGE PROTECTION AND SCHEME FOR MAXIMUM ADVANCE (SMA) COSTS

A measure of the direct housing cost of children is the value of the difference in size between a standard house for two adults and a standard house for two adults and two children. If the value of the extra space needed for child-rearing is taken as the increased level of mortgage repayment, then the cost of the children in the same house profile will only differ according to the stage reached in their parents' housing career. The most common stage reached in owner occupied housing for the families described is the established or 10-year mortgage history, which will be referred to subsequently as a 'general' standard for analysis purposes.

RENT

The additional cost of rent for families with children is also the consequence of the increase in accommodation size. The two adult family rents a one bedroom flat and the family with two children rents a three bedroom house. The children's share of the direct housing cost in the rented sector is therefore the value of the extra rental for a larger property.

INDIRECT HOUSING COSTS OF CHILDREN

CONTENTS INSURANCE

House contents insurance is included in owner occupied and local authority dwellings in this research. The owner occupied house contents insurance is included as a structural and contents insurance package, whereas the local authority 'contents' insurance is based on the best of a number of quotations for policies which provide a £30,000 cover for household effects. The amount of cover provided bears little relationship to the presence of children and is thus excluded from the child's housing standard.

WATER RATE AND SEWERAGE CHARGES

The water rates and the sewerage rates are assessed by the rateable value of the property or the most common local charge for that size of dwelling. There is little doubt that the presence of children results in additional usage of utilities to a greater degree than for extra adults in families. The difference between the two adult housing (taken as the reference point) and families with children is the child's share.

COMMUNITY CHARGE (COUNCIL TAX SINCE APRIL 1993)

The community charge and the council tax are not relative to age, number of children, or direct services to children and therefore have been discounted in the child's housing standard.

HOUSING MAINTENANCE

The level of household decoration and DIY activities according to family type is largely an unknown factor. It is possible that cost levels relate to preference and aptitude rather than to size or age of the property.

- *Internal maintenance.* The estimate for interior maintenance is based on an allowance provided to all new tenants by York Housing Department. It is assumed that children increase the need for re-decoration and repair of homes in terms of general wear and tear and the cost of decorating the children's bedrooms. The extra cost allowed for three bedroom dwellings compared to one bedroom properties is taken as the standard for children.
- *External maintenance.* The external decoration standard applies to owner occupied dwellings only and is influenced by the age and size of the property. A two tier system of costs relates to new property (lower) and older housing. Children are not considered a major factor in decisions to decorate exteriors more often.

FUEL

In general, households use fuel for heating space and water, cooking, lighting, and to drive appliances. The total fuel bill of most families, except those who use solid fuel such as coal, consists of a 'fixed' standing charge for meter rental and a charge per unit for fuel consumed.

The modest-but-adequate standard is based on the principle that people should be warm enough and comfortable in their homes. The assumptions made by the 'experts' on the amount of fuel needed take into account:

* the dwelling used for each family type (construction, dimensions, volume, heating system, number of family members);[3]
* the leisure and work related assumptions for each family type;
* the limitations of the computer model (BREDEM 8) available to calculate the family fuel standard.[4]

Table 3 shows the cost of the different components of fuel consumption. The average fuel cost for the child per year is the sum of the consumption cost of the family with children less that of the two adults. In younger two child families the average child cost is £1.28 each week in owner occupied 1980s property and £2.42 in local authority 1930s property. This represents 11% and 16% respectively of the aggregate family fuel budget. The consequence of an increase in costs to heat the teenager's study room is marginal, approximately £0.09 to £0.16 per week.

TABLE 3: **The cost of fuel for three family types, by tenure, October 1991 prices, in £s**

	Tenure	Space heat*	Water heat	Cook	Lights/ appli	year bill**	diff*** year	cost wk****
2 adult	Owner occupier	147	100	26	105	378	–	–
2 adult	Local authority	277	100	26	118	521	–	–
2 adult 2 child 4, 10	Owner occupier	133	144	26	208	511	133	1.28
2 adult 2 child 4, 10	Local authority	293	144	26	310	773	252	2.42
2 adult 2 child 10, 16	Owner occupier	142	144	26	208	520	142	1.37
2 adult 2 child 10, 16	Local authority	309	144	26	310	789	268	2.58

* See below for an explanation of why space heat costs are lower for families with children in owner occupied homes.
** Not including standing charge or annual boiler service.
*** Annual bill of the 2 adult/2 child family less the annual bill of the 2 adults.
**** Difference between families divided by 52, divided by 2 = cost of each child.

METHODS

A differential approach is taken to estimate the child's fuel cost following adjustments to the calculation used to estimate the family fuel consumptions. The adjustments are made because:

- there is a high consumption of fuel in relation to space heating in local authority homes in the child's estimate which is a consequence of volume differences between the properties compared, as shown in Table 4, and not because of the presence of children;
- the frequency that electrical appliances are used is based on adult patterns of consumption.

TABLE 4: **Comparison of dwelling volumes**

Family type	Owner occupiers	Volume (m3)	Local authority	Volume (m3)
2 adult/2 child	3 bed modern semi	179.8	3 bed 1930s end terrace	212.6
2 adult	2 bed 1890s terrace	175.2	1 bed 1930s flat	105.0
Volume difference		4.6		107.6

The adjustments to the calculation are shown below:

- In each type of tenure the energy consumption needs of the 2 adult family is estimated in the housing profile of the 2 adult/2 child family with 50% of the upstairs excluded from the calculation.
- A 50% supplement to the existing allocation of hot water and appliance usage is assigned to the children's standard.

Table 5 shows the adjusted fuel consumption for 2 adult and 2 adult/2 child in owner occupied and local authority homes. The BREDEM simulated approach adjusted the fuel consumption in the homes to reflect the different lifestyles of the families compared and to minimise the differences arising from house size variations expressed earlier in cubic metres (volume). The difference now remaining in the fuel consumption of families according to tenure is due to the differences in the dimensions of rooms and construction of materials of the specified properties utilised as model homes for families with children.

TABLE 5: **Fuel consumption for three family types, by tenure, using the BREDEM simulated approach**

	Tenure	Space heating (therm)	Water heating (therm)	Cooking (therm)	Lights and appliances (kWh)
2 adult	owner occupier	321	217	57	1367
2 adult	local authority	603	217	57	1527
2 adult/ 2 child 4,10	owner occupier	290	313	57	2696
2 adult/ 2 child 4,10	local authority	639	313	57	3097
2 adult/ 2 child 10,16	owner occupier	309	313	57	2696
2 adult/ 2 child 10,16	local authority	674	313	57	3097

FOOD

Food is the largest component in the cost of a child with the exception of child care costs. The family food budgets reflect the usual purchasing and consumption patterns of the particular family types at a modest-but-adequate standard. The budget satisfies the requirement of all family members to have enough food and Dietary Nutrient Intake (DNIs) and furthermore meets the objective of a healthy diet at a reasonable cost. Overall, the food budget standard is determined using 'expert' judgements about what family food consumption should be, and from behavioural evidence about what family food consumption is in reality.

Table 6 shows the food cost for individual family members. The food costs of children are quite considerable; they increase with age and boys cost more than girls. At age 4 a child has food costs of £9.61 or £10.02 each week, by the age of 16, costs are £16.41 or £18.44 each week, girls and boys respectively.

METHODS

Data from the *National Food Survey* (NFS) provides a diet profile of average food consumption with additions such as alcohol beverages, sweets and soft drinks, and foods eaten outside the family. The 1988 *Family Expenditure Survey* (FES) provides the basis for the estimate of sweets and soft drinks, while alcoholic drinks are based on Health Education Authority recommendations. There is an allowance for 6% food wastage, 3-5% of food allowed for consumption by visitors, and 8-25% for meals which are eaten out.

TABLE 6: **The weekly food costs of adults and children according to family type, October 1991, £ per week**

| | | FAMILY TYPE[5] | |
		2 adult/2 child, age 4/10	2 adult/2 child, age 10/16
Food			
Adult	male	20.03	20.27
	female	14.03	14.18
age 11-17	male	18.23	18.44
	female	16.23	16.41
age 5-10	male	14.63	14.79
	female	12.22	12.37
age 1-4	male	10.02	10.13
	female	9.61	9.73
Alcohol			
Adult	male	7.42	7.42
	female	5.30	5.30

In order to set the food budget at a reasonable level we used Sainsbury's food prices. The leading lines are assumed to reflect the usual or average family food purchasing patterns and to meet economy goals. The food is priced at March 1992 prices, and represents a notional estimate of the cost of the family weekly diet. A shopping basket of food can be produced by converting the notional model of the family food profiles into a shopping list of items such as whole loaves of bread, packets of biscuits, pints of milk and cuts of meat. Those items which would be replaced over a longer period of time – such as tea, coffee or marmalade – can be allocated a lifetime to give a weekly estimate of the cost.

The distribution of food among family members is calculated by a scale of 'family values' developed by Nelson,[6] which describes the allocation of food energy in particular households according to age and sex. The ratio equals the average intake of each age/sex group divided by the average intake of the adult male. The family values shown in Table 7 are applied to the NFS-derived family food profile for the family of 2 adults/2 or 3 children to estimate the child's share, and hence cost. The children's proportion is calculated from the family food profile, excluding any nutrients derived from alcohol.

The male child in all cases has higher nutrition needs than the female child. Under five years old, the difference between the sexes in DNIs is marginal. However, between the ages of 5 and 10 the dietary nutrient intake need accelerates considerably by a 0.12 'family value' and retains this difference between boys and girls into adulthood.

Table 7. **Factors (family values) used to allocate food distribution in family of 2 adults and 2/3 children**

		2 adults & 2/3 children
Adult over 18	male	1.00
	female	0.70
Child 11-17	male	0.91
	female	0.81
Child 5-10	male	0.73
	female	0.61
Child < 5	male	0.51
	female	0.48

Source: Nelson (1986)

CLOTHING

Needs for clothing arise from family activities, such as leisure, relaxation, work or school attendance, special occasions, and seasonal changes. The modest-but-adequate living standard sets the following criteria for clothes in relation to children:

- A choice of casual clothes for evenings and weekends.
- A school uniform and PE kit for school-aged children and day clothes for the child in nursery school.
- Leisure clothes for indoor and outdoor activities – for example, wellington boots, training shoes and a swimsuit.

- One smart outfit for a special occasion.
- Sufficient clothes for all seasons.

Table 8 shows that weekly clothing costs increase with the child's age ranging from £6.18 per week for a 4-year-old to £9.17 per week for a child of 16 years. The budgets for the 4-year-old of different sexes are similar; however, by the age of 10 and similarly by the age of 16, boys' clothing costs are considerably more than those for girls. In general boys' clothing budgets include fewer items but the items are inclined to be more expensive and have shorter lifespans, and this tendency increases with age. This is especially true of footwear, reflecting high cost and high replacement rates for older boys compared to girls.

TABLE 8: **Clothing costs of children by age and sex, October 1991 prices, £ per week**

	Girl 4	Boy 4	Girl 10	Boy 10*	Girl 16	Boy 16
Main items + underwear	4.93	4.60	4.60	5.33	6.64	6.05
Accessories	0.11	0.11	0.11	0.16	0.16	0.11
Footwear	1.44	1.44	2.36	2.69	1.65	2.97
Haberdashery	0.03	0.03	0.03	0.03	0.03	0.03
Total**	6.51	6.18	7.10	8.21	8.48	9.17

* full details are given in Appendix I

** differences due to rounding

METHODS

A range of factors determine the lifetime of an item of clothing. For example, consideration is given to the quality of the garment, the frequency and duration of wear, the fabric type, the manufacturing process and washing life of the garment, and the growth rate of the child. A basic clothes repair kit is included as haberdashery in the clothing standard, and the household goods and services budget includes a sewing machine for families with children.

On the whole the garments and footwear in the children's clothing budgets are basic or classic styles to facilitate pricing and replacement over a limited period of time. The children's clothing standard is made up of new clothes only – no second hand clothes are included, no 'sales clothes' are purchased, and no clothes are homemade. None of the clothing is assumed to be shared between siblings.

The selection of clothes in the children's clothing standard is made by drawing out all the individual items identified by the age and sex of the child from the modest-but-adequate database. To assess clothing standards for the opposite sex in each age group additional lists of clothing were created in a similar way.

HOUSEHOLD GOODS AND SERVICES

Household goods includes:

- Furniture, floor coverings and textiles/soft furnishings
- Gas/electric appliances, hardware and other appliances
- Stationery and paper goods
- Cleaning products
- Pet food and pet accessories

Household services includes:

- Postage and telephone costs
- Subscription fees
- Dry cleaning and shoe repairs
- Window cleaning
- Baby-sitting

Table 9 shows the total cost of household goods and services attributed to children: £5.04 for a child aged 4 years, £5.14 for a child aged 10 years, and £6.21 for a child aged 16 years. There is a small variation in costs in relation to household goods and housing tenure which is due to the amounts of floor covering and soft furnishings needed in houses of different dimensions.

METHODS

HOUSEHOLD GOODS

FURNITURE, FLOOR COVERINGS, TEXTILES AND SOFT FURNISHINGS

The capital cost of a number of commodities owned more or less exclusively by the child – eg, a child's bedroom furnishings and fittings – is included wholly in the child's standard. In other instances general furnishings and fittings are shared by all family members, thus only a very small proportion of costs is included on the grounds that these items are replaced more often where children are present. The differential calculation is used to estimate the level of wear and tear on communal household furnishings, equipment and household fabrics – ie, the cost of the lifespan difference of household goods in families with children compared to families without children. For example, the extra wear on the life of an armchair when children are present is estimated at the monetary equivalent of two years. The small difference found between children residing in local authority and owner occupied housing is entirely due to the variations in room specifications between the dwellings.

TABLE 9: **The household goods/service costs of children by age and tenure, October 1991 prices, £ per week**

	Age 4 Owner occupier	Age 4 Local authority	Age 10 Owner occupier	Age 10 Local authority	Age 16 Owner occupier	Age 16 Local authority
Household goods						
Furniture	0.86	0.86	0.86	0.86	0.87	0.87
Floor coverings	0.73	0.46	0.69	0.57	0.69	0.57
Textiles/soft furnishings	0.47	0.50	0.47	0.57	0.47	0.57
Gas, electric appliances & repairs	0.34	0.34	0.34	0.34	0.41	0.41
Kitchen & hardware	0.32	0.32	0.32	0.32	0.32	0.32
Stationery & paper goods	0.37	0.37	0.45	0.45	1.10	1.10
Toilet rolls & cleaning materials	0.61	0.61	0.61	0.61	0.61	0.61
Sub-total	**3.70**	**3.46**	**3.74**	**3.72**	**4.47**	**4.45**
Household services						
Postage	0.10	0.10	0.16	0.16	0.23	0.23
Telephone	0.00	0.00	0.00	0.00	1.06	1.06
Shoe repairs	0.00	0.00	0.00	0.00	0.19	0.19
Dry cleaning	0.00	0.00	0.00	0.00	0.22	0.22
Spare key	0.00	0.00	0.00	0.00	0.01	0.01
Passport	0.00	0.00	0.00	0.00	0.03	0.03
Baby-sitting	1.24	1.24	1.24	1.24	0.00	0.00
Sub-total	**1.34**	**1.34**	**1.40**	**1.40**	**1.74**	**1.74**
Total	**5.04**	**4.80**	**5.14**	**5.12**	**6.21**	**6.19**

GAS, ELECTRICAL SERVICES AND REPAIRS

In general the additional wear and tear and repair costs on gas and electrical equipment, kitchen and hardware goods in families with children is included in the child's standard. (The extra fuel used by children is included in the fuel budget standard.) Food mixers, microwaves and sewing machines are examples of extra items included in families with children but not in families without children. A small amount of cost which represents the child's need is included in the child's budget but these items are largely considered to contribute towards a saving in time for parents rather than just to service the needs of children.

STATIONERY AND PAPER GOODS

The items included in the child's standard are those relating to child use – eg, extra paper, pens, pencils, crayons, school equipment and Christmas cards.

TOILET PAPER AND CLEANING MATERIALS

The standard for toilet rolls is one each week per person and no distinction is made between adult and child use. However, the extra household cleaning caused by children is calculated as the additional amount of cleaning materials purchased by households which include children compared to two adult families.

PET FOOD AND PET ACCESSORIES

No part of the cost of family pets are included in the children's standard, since ownership is regarded here as a parental responsibility.

HOUSEHOLD SERVICES

The additional cost of most household services for families with children tends to be the result of the working and leisure lifestyle of the parents. Exceptions are mainly found in the budget of the child aged 16 who incurs telephone, postal and a small amount of dry cleaning and repair costs. However, baby-sitting and child care costs are substantial for younger children and are considered here as child costs rather than parent costs.

BABY-SITTING

In families with two older children aged 10 and 16 years, baby-sitting costs are assigned at a lower frequency on the assumption that the older child will share this task. The family with young children aged 4 and 10 years employ baby-sitters once every two weeks for a pre-midnight three-hour session. The family with older children use baby-sitters for a pre-midnight three-hour session every four weeks. In addition both family types use a baby-sitter for a post-midnight sit twice a year with a taxi home for the sitter as shown in Table 10.

TABLE 10: **Baby-sitting frequency and average weekly cost, October 1991 prices, £ per week**							
frequency/yr	hrs/wk	service	hour/yr	cost/hr	cost/yr	cost/wk	each child
Child 4,10 – younger family							
26	3	before 12am	78.00	1.50	117.00	2.25	
2	1	after 12am	2.00	2.50	5.00	0.10	
2	1	taxi for sitter		3.50	7.00	0.14	
Total						2.49	1.25
Child 10 – older family							
13	3	before 12am	39.00	1.50	58.50	1.13	
2	1	after 12am	2.00	2.50	5.00	0.10	
2	1	taxi for sitter		3.50	7.00	0.14	
Total						1.33	1.33

CHILD CARE

The decision to include expenditure on child care for families with working mothers in the family budgets is open to debate. Empirical evidence in the UK shows that informal (non-paid) child care is the most common arrangement overall for working mothers of young children. The 1980 *Women and Employment Survey* found that only a small percentage of working mothers used formal child care such as day nurseries, nannies and au pairs.[7] In the case of full-time work it is common to use maternal grandmothers, whereas for mothers working part-time the most common providers of child care are husbands.

Clearly the family budgets have to some extent disregarded behavioural information and have included formal as distinct from informal child care for working mothers. There are three reasons for this.

First, to include informal, unpaid child care in the budget standard might imply support for the inadequate state child care provision in the UK. Present levels of care exclude those mothers from the workforce who have no informal network of child care available to them and whose earnings are insufficient to pay for private child care. This situation increases the 'opportunity costs' of child-rearing and restricts choice and equal opportunity for working women.

Second, informal child care resources are not necessarily 'free'. Although the frequency and level of charges made by relatives and friends is largely unknown – eg, payment in cash in hand or in exchange for services – these informal arrangements carry some cost.

Third, adopting a formal child care standard has the advantage of using a known price base, which is equally available to all family types regardless of unknown factors such as the existence of an informal network of care by grandparents. Childminders are the dominant form of paid child care in the UK; the rate used is the 'minimum' pay suggested by the National Childminders Association in October 1991.

The cost of child care varies according to the number of hours of care needed exclusive of school and nursery hours, and the total annual holiday period of the working parent. It is assumed that the child aged 4 attends the infant class of the local state primary school. (In addition some after-school care is needed for the child aged 10 if the mother works full-time.) Extra hours are included for the school holidays for both young children. Families with children aged 4 and 10 years old requiring part-time child care hours have average costs of £22.86 each week. For families where the mother works full-time, the average child care costs are £56.54 each week as shown in Table 11.

TABLE 11: **Child care**

Part-time = child care for 21 hours a week including travel time, 47 weeks a year
Full-time = child care for 42.75 hours a week including travel, 47 weeks a year

work status of mother	aged 4	aged 10	aged 16
full-time work	39.36	17.18	0.00
part-time work	18.01	4.85	0.00

Rates: £1.30 per hour, after school and school holiday rate £1.50 per hour

TRANSPORT

Family spending on transport can be explained in terms of different family circumstances, preferences and living standards. For example, the location of home in relation to shops, schools, work or leisure facilities; ownership of private transport; availability of an adequate public transport system; general health or attitude of the family towards other modes of travel, such as cycling, walking or private hire of transport.

The family transport budget includes public transport costs, bicycle costs, and private car ownership costs of a modest five-year-old car. The annual travel mileage for the two adults and two children family and the two adult families is approximately 9,000 to 10,000 miles per year.

The weekly transport costs for a child are shown in Table 12. They range from £4.68 for a child aged 4 to £5.85 for a child aged 16.

METHODS

MOTORING

In this budget children incur not only public transport costs which are relatively simple to identify, but also some costs relating to private car ownership. Children lead to extra costs for car-owning families in two different ways:

- If the number or presence of children is the reason for families buying a larger or additional car, then the 'differential' cost between a large and a small car or a second car is clearly the direct cost of the child. In the case of the two parent and two child family a larger car is needed for four

people. The extra cost includes the differential cost of depreciation insurance and servicing.
• The cost of extra mileage on child–related journeys. The cost of each car mile in relation to children takes account of the capacity of the car in miles per gallon, cost of petrol, oil, tyres and servicing.

TABLE 12: **Transport costs for children by age, October 1991 prices, £ per week**

Family expenditure	Child calculations	Aged 4	Aged 10	Aged 16
Car depreciation	Differential cost Escort-Fiesta	0.63	0.63	0.63
Car insurance	Differential cost Escort-Fiesta	0.51	0.51	0.15
Child car mileage	Petrol + oil + tyre + servicing	1.11	1.11	1.76
Car safety seat	£15.00 life 2/yrs	0.14	0.00	0.00
Sub-total		**2.39**	**2.25**	**2.54**
Public transport by train	Family rail card + one fare + Apex fare	0.00	1.38	0.60
Public transport by bus	Accompanying parent: 1 return journey wk + reduced rate child 4 or 10 & 16 year adult fare	2.10	0.70	1.40
Taxi fares	Age 4 & 10: two each year Age 16: four each year	0.19	0.19	0.39
Bicycle – capital cost	Value £149.99 – lifespan 10 years	0.00	0.00	0.29
Bicycle maintenance cost	Tyres, tubes, oil, repair kit, brake blocks + lights & batteries	0.00	0.00	0.52
Bicycle safety equipment	Safety helmet life 10 years safety harness life 5 years bike lock life 10 years	0.00	0.00	0.11
Sub-total		**2.29**	**2.27**	**3.31**
Total transport		**4.68**	**4.52**	**5.85**

The frequency of child-related journeys is calculated as a third of business and personal mileage, a third of leisure miles, and a per capita share of the annual holiday mileage. This results in 1,692 car miles and 210 public transport miles per year. In addition, the teenager is assigned an extra 500 miles per year to account for the extra journeys incurred by parents on their behalf, such as ferrying children to and from events.

PUBLIC TRANSPORT

The cost of using public transport for children is dependent on the child's age. (The child aged 16 years pays an adult fare, the child aged 10 years pays a reduced fare, and the child aged 4 travels free on train journeys and some local buses.) The young child is assumed to travel accompanied by a parent (or childminder) and this fare is included in the child's budget. However, there are no school transport costs included for the 10 year old who walks to the local school, or for the child aged 16 who is likely to cycle or walk. In general the child's public transport standard includes a minimum of one journey on the local bus with a parent where appropriate, each week, and a return long-distance train journey (York to London) each year.

BICYCLE

The bicycle owned by the 16-year-old is a new Apollo Arizona valued at £149.99. The bicycle is given a 10-year lifespan to calculate depreciation costs, and the budget includes maintenance costs, lights and batteries, and bicycle safety equipment such as a safety helmet, harness and a bike lock. Details of the bicycles owned by the children aged 10 and 4 are found in Appendix 2.

TAXIS

The standard includes annually two taxi fares per adult for leisure or personal business, two taxis each for the children aged 4 and 10, and four taxi fares for the 16-year-old for late-night entertainment.

LEISURE GOODS AND SERVICES

Leisure goods and services are a crucial component of the costs of a child. They provide the breadth of activity and experience for a child's full development. A summary of the leisure goods and services budget for children aged 4, 10, and 16, is shown in Table 13. Leisure goods and services costs for children increase with age. At age 4 years the total cost each week is £5.82 of which £2.06 is related to toys, games or hobbies. At age 10 years the largest cost is still toys, games and hobbies and the total cost each week £7.21. By the age of 16 years the total budget is £9.56 which includes substantial sports, entertainment, holiday and book costs.

TABLE 13: **Leisure goods and services costs for children by age. October 1991 prices, £ per week**

	Child 4	Child 10	Child 16
Leisure goods			
Television, video & audio equipment and repairs	0.74	0.41	1.13
Sports goods	0.03	0.07	0.04
Books, newspapers, magazines	0.29	1.01	1.39
Toys, games and hobbies*	2.06	2.04	0.27
Seasonal items	0.17	0.15	0.15
Photographic equipment and processing	0.11	0.26	0.61
Total	**3.40**	**3.94**	**3.59**
Leisure services			
Sports expenses	0.00	0.85	1.10
Arts/entertainment/outings	0.26	0.40	1.51
School/club	1.21	0.93	0.69
Holiday expenses	0.95	1.09	2.67
Total	**2.42**	**3.27**	**5.97**
Total goods and services	**5.82**	**7.21**	**9.56**

* for full details see Appendix 2

METHODS

LEISURE GOODS

The child's 'leisure goods standard' includes sporting equipment, toys, games, and books, which develop physical and creative skills. The standard includes items owned by the particular child, such as toys, and a proportion of items part owned, such as family games, Christmas crackers and fireworks. In addition the 'differential' approach identifies the extra costs of common items in families with children compared to those families without children – eg, the extra wear and tear caused by children which results in early replacement of goods, or the cost of increases in the frequency of repairs for home entertainment equipment.

LEISURE SERVICES

The family leisure activities in the FBU budget are based on a model of the most popular adult pastimes recorded in the GHS *General Household Survey 1987*[8] (provided they meet the criteria of modest-but-adequate in expenditure and cultural expectations), and an estimation of frequency based on the amount of free time available to partake recorded by the Henley Centre.[9] The result is multiplied by the cost of the activity to provide a weekly estimate of leisure service costs for each family.

The family standard is founded on adult leisure behaviour and so the following principles are applied to formulate a children's leisure services standard:

- The teenage child is classed as an adult.
- The mother is assumed to accompany the younger child in all the child's leisure activities, and therefore in certain sports the participation rate of the child is similar to that of the mother. The criteria for including children in the parent's leisure services is that the activities can be *either*
  - fully shared activities with a parent, such as walking, swimming or football and therefore a similar frequency rate as the mother, *or*
  - partly shared activities with a parent, for example, going to the cinema, which the mother and child may do together, or the mother can go alone as part of her free time. In this case an arbitrary frequency rate for a child's activity is given as 50% of a mother's rate.
- Some additional child-related activities are included in the budget

standard where parents are involved only at the margins – eg, cub scouts or 'Tumble Tots' sessions.

Football is included as a popular spectator sport. Other social or family activities include dancing, the cinema and, to a lesser degree, shows, pantomimes and exhibitions. Day trips, local trips and holiday entertainment include visits to the Tower of London, the National Photography Museum in Bradford, York Minster and Blackpool Tower. The most popular UK holiday varies according to family type – the family with children have a seven-day holiday in Blackpool, at half board rates. A number of school activities are included in the budget standard of children – eg, an excursion to Germany, a cub-scout camp, and day trips.

PERSONAL CARE

The personal care budget for a child is small compared with other component parts of the child's budget standard and in relation to the personal care expenditure of adults. The four main areas of expenditure are categorised as follows:

- Health care
- Personal hygiene
- Personal accessories
- Cosmetics

Within the UK National Health Service and the Family Health Services Authority, children below the age of 16, and in some cases older, are entitled to free health care. This includes consultations, medication and treatment, in-patient and out-patient hospital care, dental care (prevention of cavities and treatment) and ophthalmic care (regular eye examination and supplying of spectacles).

Personal hygiene items result in the highest expenditure in the personal care standard for children of all ages and this increases two and three-fold between the ages of 10 and 16 years, as shown in Table 14. Under the age of 11 years, the personal care budget does not vary according to age or sex. At 16 years, however, the teenage girl costs £1.08 or 30% more each week than a teenage boy in terms of personal hygiene, personal accessories and cosmetics as shown in the table below:

Table 14: **Personal care costs of children by age and sex, October 1991 prices, £ per week**

	Aged 4 male/female	Aged 10 male/female	Aged 16 male	Aged 16 female
Health care	0.11	0.11	0.14	0.14
Personal hygiene	0.79	0.79	1.87	2.39
Personal accessories	0.07	0.07	0.38	0.52
Cosmetics	0.00	0.00	0.16	0.57
Total	0.97	0.97	2.55	3.62

METHODS

The differential method is used to assign extra quantities of personal care items to the child's budget. These extras are identified by the shorter lifetimes on commodities in families with two adults and two children when compared to families without children – eg, soap and toothpaste. Additional items are included which are appropriate in terms of sex, age and price – eg, cough mixture, creams and first aid supplies, haircuts and hair brushes, school bags, sunglasses, and cosmetics such as aftershave and skin cleansers.

POCKET MONEY

Pocket money is shown as a separate component in the child's budget standard for very good reasons. Parents give pocket money to their children as part of a deeply held tradition – for example, it has been suggested adult habits of using money for spending, gambling and saving are established early in childhood.[10] Similarly, it has also been found that pocket money is linked to moral and educational development from an early age.[11] The sum included is free standing and not accounted for in the budget standard of the family.[12]

The pocket money is based on average amounts reported in the Wall's Pocket Money Monitor;[13] it varies by the age of the child as follows:

- Child aged 4   =   £0.30 per week

- Child aged 10 = £1.43 per week
- Child aged 16 = £2.89 per week

As a proportion of the child's overall budget standard, the pocket money element represents a budget share of 5% for the teenager, 3% for the child aged 10 years and less than 1% for the child aged 4 years.

NOTES

1   The families are allocated local authority rented accommodation. The York Housing Services Department policy is to allocate three bedroom houses to families with children of different sexes, whereas two adult families would be housed in a one bedroom flat.

2   Normative judgements and behavioural information are used to assess the purchase price, term of mortgage, and level of deposit in relation to owner occupied housing. The owner occupiers are mortgage holders. The mortgage for two adults and families with children is based on 25 years repayment at two points in the housing career: first time buyers and established ten-year history of buying. Monthly repayments are net of tax relief on interest at the 25% rate, and include the cost of a decreasing term mortgage protection premium, and other costs associated with lending where it exceeds 75% of the purchase price. An estimated total of £1,000 is included to cover legal fees, survey reports and stamp duty. Additional housing costs included in the family housing budget are: structural and contents insurance, water and sewerage rates, community charge, and housing decoration and repair.

3   The families have a whole-house balanced flue gas central heating system. The insulation and lagging of the hot water tank, and the ventilation rate are taken as a middle range value. The temperatures of the homes differ according to use of rooms. The downstairs living accommodation is set to maintain a temperature of 21°C, and the upstairs area is set to 18°C during heat 'on' periods. This temperature is increased to a mean temperature upstairs of 19°C to 'draw off' a 21°C environment in the teenager's study bedroom. The central heating 'on' periods are limited by the family's work, leisure and child care patterns, within a range of 9 to 16 hours a day.

4   The range of electrical appliances included in each family is specified according to family needs, but the frequency the appliances are used is constrained by the 'BREDEM 8' computer program. BREDEM weights appliance usage by adult use estimated in accordance with research carried out in the early 1980s.

5   Food costs for the original two child family are estimated from the *National Food Survey* for families of two or three children, and a ratio of the distribution of nutrients and energy in specific families. No account can therefore be taken of further costs or savings incurred by different sized families in this particular study.

6   M Nelson, 'The Distribution of Nutrient Intake within Families', *British Journal of Nutrition* 55, 1986, pp267-77

7   Cited in B Cohen, *Caring for Children, Services and Policies for Childcare and Equal Opportunities in the UK*, Family Policy Studies Centre, 1988, p18

8   Office of Population Censuses and Surveys, *General Household Survey 1987 Supplement: Participation in Sport*, HMSO, 1990

9   Henley Centre 'Time Budgets', *Leisure Futures*, November 1991.

10   A Furnham and A Lewis, *Economic Mind: The Social Psychology of Economic Behaviour*, Wheatsheaf, 1986

11   M Hill, 'Children's Roles in the Domestic Economy', *Journal of Consumer Studies and Home Economics* 16, 1992, pp33-50

12   The family budgets from which these children's budgets are derived consider 'spending money' as an *intra-household transfer*. For example, children's pocket money, earnings and handouts from within and outside the family, is spent as a family transaction on items already counted in the component parts of the family budgets. Sweets and crisps are included in the food budget, and small games, pencils or comics are included in the leisure standard. It is evident from this perspective that income to sustain spending in the children's leisure, clothing or food standards may be partly the children's own. A notional pocket money estimate was made by counting small items and items typically bought with pocket money and found to be in the range of 63 pence for the child aged 4 years, £1.55 for the child aged 10 years and £6.00 each week for the child aged 16. These amounts are not shown separately in the child budget standard because of double counting.

13   Birds Eye Wall's Ltd, *Wall's Pocket Money Monitor*, 1991

3 Summary: modest-but-adequate budgets

The weekly costs of boys and girls is shown in Table 15 at April 1993 prices. The overall average weekly costs of a child in owner occupied housing at the age of 4 years is £62.35, at the age of 10 years £56.02 and at the age of 16 years £65.26. (The reason for the drop in costs from 4 years to 10 years is the reduction in child care costs, which are higher for the pre-school child.) If housing costs are excluded from the child's budget standard, then children aged 4, 10 and 16 years will have costs of £55.29, £48.96 and £58.20 respectively. The overall weekly costs for children in local authority tenure are similar. At aged 4 years a child costs £62.20, at aged 10 years £56.09 and at the age of 16 years £65.40. Excluding housing costs the children's costs are reduced to £56.18, £50.07 and £59.38 for children aged 4, 10 and 16 years respectively. The largest weekly expenditure in the pre-school aged child's budget regardless of tenure is for child care, which accounts of more than 31% of the total, but this decreases with age as the hourly need for care declines. For all children food, clothing and housing present major costs.

The cost of a child increases with age. If child care costs are excluded, a boy aged 16 years in owner occupied housing costs £13.46 more than a boy aged 10, and a boy aged 10 years costs £9.60 more than a boy aged 4 years. Food, clothing, leisure and pocket money costs increase with the age of the child, while personal care and fuel costs are similar for younger children under 11 years, but they increase for the teenage child.

Boys are more expensive than girls. At 4 years old the difference is small, but for older children aged 10 and 16, the cost is £3.67 more for a 10 year old boy than for a girl, and £1.66 each week more for a boy of 16 years old than for a girl of the same age. The original family budgets include toys, leisure goods, and some clothes that are gender neutral; however, other clothing, personal care and food are found to differ in cost, quantity, or particular items according to the sex of the child. For example, boys aged 10 and 16 years have higher food costs than girls of the same age – £2.54 and £2.13 respectively each week, because of greater nutrient need.

TABLE 15: **The cost of a child by age and sex, April 1993 prices, £ per week**

Owner occupied tenure

Commodity	Boy 4	Girl 4	Boy 10	Girl 10	Boy 16	Girl 16
Housing	7.06	7.06	7.06	7.06	7.06	7.06
Fuel	1.26	1.26	1.26	1.26	1.35	1.35
Food	10.53	10.10	15.38	12.84	19.38	17.25
Clothing	6.26	6.59	8.32	7.19	9.29	8.60
Household g/s	5.24	5.24	5.35	5.35	6.41	6.41
Child care p/t	19.37	19.37	5.22	5.22	0.00	0.00
Motoring	2.57	2.57	2.42	2.42	2.73	2.73
Fares	2.49	2.49	2.53	2.53	3.60	3.60
Leisure	2.68	2.68	3.60	3.60	6.59	6.59
Leisure goods	3.58	3.58	4.17	4.17	3.94	3.94
Pocket money	0.31	0.31	1.49	1.49	3.01	3.01
Personal care	1.05	1.05	1.05	1.05	2.73	3.89
Total	**62.40**	**62.30**	**57.85**	**54.18**	**66.09**	**64.43**
Total less child care cost	43.03	42.93	52.63	48.96	66.09	64.43
Total less housing costs	55.34	55.24	50.79	47.12	59.03	57.37
Total less child care and housing	35.97	35.87	45.57	41.90	59.03	57.37
Local authority tenure						
Total	**62.25**	**62.15**	**57.92**	**54.25**	**66.23**	**64.57**
Less housing	**56.23**	**56.13**	**51.90**	**48.23**	**60.21**	**58.55**

In 1993 there was no significant difference in costs between a child living in different tenure – approximately £1.00. However, the picture was different in 1991 when the budgets were first created. A child's share of the rent in local authority housing was 36% less than the child's share of the mortgage in owner occupied housing. In 1993 this percentage difference was 15. This was due to the deflation that occurred as a result of the instability of the housing market. Incidentally, fuel costs are found to be higher in local authority than owner occupied housing – £1.13 more for a child under 11 and £1.20 more for a child aged 16. The difference in cost is probably due to the age and construction of the properties rather than the form of tenure itself.

The cost of children varies not only according to the age and sex of the child, but also in relation to family size. The original family data from which the child costs are derived was collected for the purpose of estimating costs in two child families. But it is possible to approximate the cost of a child in a *one*-child family from this data. The term 'economies of scale' is used here to describe the difference in costs for additional children in the family. Parts of the child's budget standard such as housing, private transport, household services, leisure services and food have major elements of shared cost and so potential for economies of scale. Table 16 shows that economies of scale are greatest in relation to housing costs for children of all ages and substantial for baby-sitting costs for young children. Overall, economies of scale result in additional costs of £8.50 or £7.44 per week for a child in a *one*-child family aged either 4 or 10, and £7.17 or £6.11 for the only child aged 16 in owner occupied and local authority tenure respectively.

TABLE 16: **Extra costs for a child in a one child family, by age and tenure, April 1993 prices, £ per week**

	Child aged 4		Child aged 10		Child aged 16	
	O/O	LA	O/O	LA	O/O	LA
Housing	5.86	4.80	5.86	4.80	5.86	4.80
Household services baby-sitting	1.33	1.33	1.33	1.33	0.00	0.00
Leisure	0.13	0.13	0.13	0.13	0.13	0.13
Motoring	1.18	1.18	1.18	1.18	1.18	1.18
Total extra costs	8.50	7.44	8.50	7.44	7.17	6.11

O/O owner occupied
LA local authority

4 Low cost budget standard for a child

A low cost budget has been devised to inform the debate about the adequacy of the child scale rates in income support, child benefit, family credit and the Child Support Agency's formula. This budget is based on a list of items which people should not have to do without – such as adequate health care, a healthy diet, warm shelter with enough space for each family member and the opportunity to participate in community activities.

The low cost budget is derived by scaling down modest-but-adequate budget standards so that they reflect a low cost standard of living. This process depends upon adjusting four variables:

- the selection of items for inclusion in the list,
- the quantity selected of each item and the lifetime allocated,
- the quality of the selected items, *and*
- the pricing method.

A lower standard of living can be reflected by narrowing the range of items to be included, or by reducing the quantity of each item. As with the modest-but-adequate budget, these choices are informed by ownership rates. Only items owned by 75% or more of the population are included in the low cost budget. In addition, the budget is informed by evidence of what the general public consider to be necessities. If two-thirds or more of the public believe that any particular item is a necessity, it is included in the budget.[1] Where less than two-thirds of the population believe an item to be a necessity, the item is still included if it nevertheless meets the 75% ownership criterion.

Budgets can also be reduced by extending the assumed lifetimes of items or by using cheaper brands or retailers. However, cheaper prices have been avoided where the eventual trade off between price, quality and lifetime is likely to increase long-term costs.

Low cost budgets have been constructed for a number of different family types,[2] both with and without children. Here we look at two of these family types: a two adult family without children (2 adult) and the two adult with two children (2 adult/2 child) family – a boy aged 10 and a girl aged 4. Both adults in the childless couple are assumed to be working full-time for low incomes. Of the adults in the family with children, the man is assumed to be in full-time low-wage employment, whereas the woman is assumed not to be in paid work. There is no allowance for child care costs or for costs of transport to school in the low cost budget. We also look at a lone parent family with two children as part of a comparison of benefits and low cost budgets.

The low cost budget is calculated by constructing detailed baskets of goods and services for eight components and then adding together the costs of each of the these components of the budget. The low cost child budget is derived by a differential method (see p9).

Although the cost of a child is calculated by this differential method, the result still takes into account the individual needs of each child. This is because the 2 adult/2 child family budget is calculated using individual consumptions in the components such as clothing, personal care, transport, leisure services, and some leisure goods and household goods and services in which items for the children can be easily identified. The other components in the budgets – housing, fuel and food – need not be treated in this way, as joint consumption is a dominant factor in determining the costs of these components.

LOW COST BUDGET COMPONENTS

HOUSING

The modest-but-adequate housing profiles for local authority tenants are adopted in constructing the low cost housing budget. This is for three reasons:

- It is more realistic to adopt rented housing for a low cost housing budget.
- The local authority three bedroomed terraced house is a reasonable basic standard for a low cost budget, as the amount of space for each member meets minimum standards.[3]
- The selected types and locations of local authority housing are among the most common kinds of housing in the survey area – York.

The housing cost of children is the differential cost (see p9) and includes rent, water and sewerage charges, internal maintenance and contents insurance. Rent, water and sewerage charges are the same for both low cost and modest-but-adequate standards. Internal decoration costs are reduced to about one-tenth of the modest-but-adequate standards, on the assumption that decoration work will be carried out every ten years. No external maintenance costs are included in the low cost housing budget because the council is assumed to be responsible for the structural maintenance of local authority accommodation.

FUEL

The low cost fuel standard aims to set budgets for an adequate quality of life, adequate for the maintenance of a healthy lifestyle, but affordable to families on low incomes. To reduce fuel costs, a lower demand temperature than the modest-but-adequate standard is set (20°C) in the living area, but the same temperature (18°C) is adopted for the children's bedroom. A gas central heating system is allocated for the low cost energy standard because of its high energy efficiency. Nevertheless, the fuel budgets do not include the capital costs of installation of such a system.

The low cost fuel budget is higher than the modest-but-adequate fuel budget for two reasons:

• The heating times are extended beyond those of the modest-but-adequate budget. This is primarily because the mother who is not in paid work is assumed to stay at home to look after the children, and the children are more likely to stay at home throughout the day than the higher income earning families reflected in the modest-but-adequate budget standards.
• Higher ventilation values are used on the basis that low income families are more likely to be living in less energy efficient dwellings.

FOOD

Because food is consumed jointly by all members of the family, food costs provide an opportunity for larger families to benefit from economies of scale. The food budget of the children is, therefore, simply the differential costs of the 2 adult/2 child and 2 adult families.

The low cost family food standard is primarily based on the modest-but-adequate food standard which is in turn derived from current patterns of food purchasing behaviour with minor amendments made to avoid an unhealthy diet. This standard is adopted so that the low cost standard ensures that there is an opportunity for the children in the family to have a healthy diet, and that the food baskets which are allocated are acceptable to most people.

To reduce the food costs, alcohol, and food eaten away from home are not included in the low cost family food budget. The costs of home food purchases are therefore increased to replace the allowance made in the modest-but-adequate budget for food eaten away from home.

Pricing for the low cost food budgets is based upon the modest-but-adequate data. The leading lines sold at Sainsbury's, most of which are also 'own brand' items, were used for pricing. According to Sainsbury's, the most popular items are generally in the cheapest price range.

CLOTHING

The low cost clothing wardrobe is a more limited one than the modest-but-adequate budget and is based on Bradshaw and Morgan's minimum wardrobe standard for children.[4] Appendix 3 shows the clothing standards (stock and quantities) for a girl aged 4 and a boy aged 10. The low cost clothing budget includes four components: outerwear, underwear and nightwear, accessories, and footwear. Some adjustments have been made to the selected items. For example, a pair of slippers is added for the 10-year-old boy, and a pair of jeans is included to replace one of the three pairs of trousers.

This low cost wardrobe is assumed to cover a basic standard including clothing required at school, at home and for social activities. Nevertheless, these baskets do not include special clothing for any particular sport. Neither do they include school uniforms or PE clothes. It is assumed that in general boys aged 10 and girls aged 4 do not need a school uniform. In addition, if families are entitled to income support or family credit, they might be able to receive assistance for school uniforms.

The clothing budgets do not take into account the fact that clothes might be passed down to the children from older brothers or sisters or from relatives or friends. This is because it is unreasonable to assume that clothing will be passed down where children are of different sexes unless the ages involved are much less than those assumed for the given family types. The clothing items were priced at C&A and British Home Stores – retailers targeted at less affluent families. Second-hand clothing is not considered in the budgets. However, the cheapest (including any sales) prices available during the pricing period were used to reduce the costs.

HOUSEHOLD GOODS AND SERVICES

There are fewer items in the low cost household goods budget than in the modest-but-adequate budget once the ownership and social acceptance criteria have been applied (see p37). Examples of goods which are excluded are the microwave, freezer and sewing machine. In addition, only the living rooms and bedrooms are carpeted; the halls/stairs and landings, kitchens and bathrooms are not. No pets are allowed for the children.

Decreased quantities and longer lifetimes are used for some of the items. For example, the lifetimes of some soft furnishings, gas and electric appliances, kitchenware and household services have been extended. Furniture list items have also been extended by five years for the adults' room but remain the same as the lifetimes in the modest-but-adequate budget for the children's room.

The low cost household goods costs for children are mainly due to the extra capital costs of furniture, floor coverings, textiles and soft furnishings for the children's rooms. The use of more communal space also increases the general household furnishing costs, even though the presence of children has only a small effect on the cost of furniture, floor coverings, and gas and electric goods in these areas.

The low cost household services budget for the families with children only includes postage (though only second class), telephone expenses, footwear repairs, dry cleaning and union membership costs. Items such as baby sitting, window cleaning, passport costs and key cutting are excluded in the low cost budget. There is no difference in the cost of these for families with children and those without.

PERSONAL CARE

The low cost personal care budget comprises three parts:

• Health care
• Personal hygiene
• Personal accessories

Cosmetics are not included in the low cost budget.

Health care costs for a child are assumed to be covered by free care from the National Health Service, although a few medical products, such as junior paracetamol and junior cough mixture, and a first aid kit are included in the low cost health care budget.

All the modest-but-adequate items are included in the low cost personal hygiene budget as the modest-but-adequate personal hygiene standard is already set at a basic level. Professional haircutting services are only provided for adults, and these are less frequent than in the modest-but-adequate standard. Since no professional haircutting service is included for the children, a home haircutting set is included for the families with children.

Personal accessories such as children's backpacks, clocks and travel goods are included. Cheapest brands are used wherever available for the selected items in the low cost standard. The popular brand items in the modest-but-adequate standard are therefore replaced with Boots own brands, thereby reducing the cost of the basket of goods.

As a result the low cost personal care budget for a child only constitutes a very small part of the overall budget mainly relating to extra toiletries and individual personal care items such as a tooth brush, hair brush, and a home haircutting set for children.

TRANSPORT

The families in the low cost budget are assumed to be non-car owners reliant on public transport as the least costly type of transportation. So the low cost budget for the children is calculated using fares for travel on local buses. The number of journeys is primarily based on behavioural data of non-car owners drawn from the *National Transport Survey*,[5] *Transport Statistics Great Britain 1978-1988*[6] and *Transport Statistics Great Britain 1991*.[7] Bus fares for two journeys a week (one return ticket) are allocated to the boy aged 10. The girl is assumed to be able to travel free on local buses due to her young age. As the children are assumed to be going to local schools, no travelling costs are allocated in connection with this.

LEISURE GOODS AND SERVICES

Leisure budgets have not traditionally been given the same level of importance as components such as food, housing and clothing, and are therefore more likely to be seen as borderline necessities, particularly within the context of setting a low cost standard of living. However, they are essential in maintaining a child's healthy life. Leisure contributes to the quality of life, offering the children and the family not only entertainment but also opportunities for social interaction.

The low cost leisure component is in two parts: leisure goods and leisure services. Leisure goods are included only if they meet the inclusion criteria – ie, that over 75% of the population have these items. These include a telephone, radio/cassette player, colour television, and video cassette recorder and video hire films. The latter may be considered a luxury. However, given how little low income families have to spend on other forms of entertainment and how home based their leisure time,[8] a video player is a very valuable commodity.

Toys, games and a small number of children's books are also included. Items in the toy list are reduced to half the number of the modest-but-adequate budget. As information about toy ownership is not available, the list can only be based on entirely normative judgement. To maintain this low cost basket of toys, £0.89 and £1.21 (April 1993 prices) per week is required for the girl aged 4 and the boy aged 10 respectively.

Although bicycles are relatively expensive items, they are included in the basket of toys for both children. This is partly in recognition of the popularity of the bicycle both as a toy and for recreational purposes and also because its inclusion can to some extent compensate for the limited travelling costs allocated to the low cost transport budget for the family with children. Bicycles are also good value for money, in that they can be expected to have a lifetime of at least four years.

The low cost leisure services budget includes the cost of two visits to the cinema per year. No allowance is made for other entertainments. It is assumed that the family will also make use of other free leisure services such as community organised activities, visiting museums and places of historic interest and using the local library. An allowance for sports and physical exercise is included for the children, based on a sports and physical exercise profile which is itself based on the popularity of individual sports and exercises among adults in the *General Household Survey*.[9] It is assumed that the children will participate in these selected activities as part of a family activity. In this case, swimming is selected, at a cost of £0.46 per week for the boy but at no cost for the girl who is assumed to be able to access the services free of charge.

No annual holiday is included; neither are school trips, scout trips nor scout camps. One day trip to Blackpool is allocated to each of the members of the family per year. An excursion organised by a local bus company is chosen as this is the cheapest travel option available.

POCKET MONEY AND CHILD CARE COSTS

Pocket money is not included as a separate item in either the low cost or modest-but-adequate family budgets as it is regarded as an intra-household expense, so that it is assumed to be spent by children on one or more of the other components such as leisure, clothing or food. However, pocket money is identified in the modest-but-adequate child budget and is estimated as £0.63 for aged 4 and £1.55 per week for aged 10 in 1991. To avoid double counting, this pocket money will not be taken into account to calculate the overall low cost child budget.

Child care costs for the children aged under 11 are not included in the summary low cost budget as the mother is assumed not to be in paid work.

NOTES

1 H Frayman, *Breadline Britain 1990s*, Domino Films/London Weekend Television, 1991
2 A C S Yu, *Low Cost Budget Standards for Three Household Types*, Working Paper 17, Family Budget Unit, University of York, 1992
3 See M Parker, *Homes for Today and Tomorrow*, HMSO, 1961 and *General Household Survey* 'bedroom standard' definition.
4 J Bradshaw and J Morgan, *Budgeting on Benefit*, Family Policy Studies Centre, 1987
5 Department of Transport, *National Travel Survey: 1985-6 Report – Part One, an Analysis of Personal Travel*, HMSO, 1988
6 Department of Transport, *Transport Statistics Great Britain 1978-88*, HMSO, 1989
7 Department of Transport, *Transport Statistics Great Britain 1991*, HMSO, 1991
8 J Bradshaw and H Holmes, *Living on the Edge*, CPAG Ltd, 1989
9 OPCS, *Participation in Sport* supplement, 1990

5 Summary: low cost budgets

Table 17 gives examples of some of the items allocated for the two children in the 2 adult/2 child family, and the summary low cost budget for a child (based upon an average of the two children) aged under 11 years. The low cost budget for a child aged under 11 is £30.37 per week – £25.23 per week after excluding housing costs.

Detailed low cost budgets for children of other ages have not been calculated. For comparison purposes, a low cost budget for a child aged 16, is estimated by using a scaling ratio which was derived from the modest-but-adequate cost of a child discussed earlier. In the modest-but-adequate budget standard, the average weekly cost of a child aged 4 to 10 was 69% of a child aged 16. Table 18 compares the low cost budget for a child aged under 11 and a child aged 16.

TABLE 17: **Basket of goods and services for the children, and the budgets for a child in the 2 adult/2 child family, £ per week, April 1993 prices**

	Basket of goods and services for the two children	Average cost of a child under 11 (£)
Housing*	2 extra bedrooms plus hall and large back garden	5.14
Fuel	Fuel use for the extra space heating and longer heating time because the house is occupied by the non-working mother and the young children	3.84
Food	Food for children	10.21
Clothing	Clothing and footwear for children	4.12
Household goods and services	Extra cleaning material, shorter lifetime of household furniture, and soft furnishings such as bedclothes and furniture for children's bedrooms	3.95
Personal care	Extra toiletries and individual personal care items for children, such as tooth brush, hair brush, and a hair cut kit for children	0.45
Transport	Bus fares for children	0.27
Leisure goods and services	Children's bikes, toys, games, books and individual leisure expenses for children including going to the movies and a day trip to Blackpool	2.38
Total**		**30.37**
Total less housing		**25.23**
Total less rent		**25.62**

* Housing costs include rent, water and sewerage charges, internal maintenance, and contents insurance

** Due to rounding, totals may not add up to the sum of their component parts

TABLE 18: **Low cost budgets for a child aged under 11 and aged 16, April 1993 prices, £ per week**

Age of child	Including housing*	Excluding housing*
Under 11	£30.37	£25.23
16	£41.71	£36.57

* Housing costs for a child aged under 11 and aged 16 are £5.14 per week

6 A comparison of low cost and modest-but-adequate budget standards

Fewer items are included for each child in the low cost budget than in the modest-but-adequate standard. Examples of items included in both these budgets are shown in Table 19. Table 20 compares the costs of a child aged under 11 for each type of budget.

The low cost budget for a child aged under 11 years is around half the modest-but-adequate budget, the total budget being 51% of the total modest-but-adequate budget when housing is included, and 48% when housing is excluded. Although child care constitutes the biggest element in the modest-but-adequate standard (23%), there is no allowance for child care in the low cost budget. If child care costs were included in the low cost budget, this budget would become almost three quarters the size of the total modest-but-adequate budget (74%).

Although most of the low cost component costs are lower than the modest-but-adequate ones, it is interesting that the fuel and the household goods and services budgets are higher. The low cost fuel budget is more expensive than the modest-but-adequate fuel budget because low income families are more likely to live in less energy efficient homes. Indeed, because of the likely energy inefficiency of the low income family's home, a slightly lower room temperature (1°C lower in the living area) is all that is maintained despite the higher fuel costs. Also, the heating period required in the low cost budget is longer, as the house is occupied by the non-working mother and the children.

TABLE 19: **Examples of budgets items included in the low cost and modest-but-adequate standard of living of children**

Low cost standard	Modest-but-adequate standard
Local authority 3 bedroomed accommodation	Local authority 3 bedroomed accommodation
Heating temperature downstairs 20°C	Heating temperature downstairs 21°C
No eating out	Eating out
Fridge, washing machine, lawn mower, vacuum cleaner	Fridge/freezer, washing machine, lawn mower, vacuum cleaner, microwave, food-mixer, sewing machine
Telephone, TV, video hire, cassette player, camera	Telephone, TV, video hire, music system, cassette player, camera
21 and 17 main clothing items for the girl (4 years) and the boy (10 years) respectively	37 and 35 main clothing items for the girl and the boy respectively
Annual footwear for the boy: 2 pairs of shoes, a pair of slippers and pumps	Annual footwear for the boy: 4 pairs of shoes, 2 pairs of trainers and pumps, 2 pairs of canvas plimsolls, a pair of slippers
Children's bicycles 1 return local bus journey a week	5-year-old family car, children's bicycles, 1 return local bus journey a week, 1 return trip to London a year, 8 taxi trips for the family
Annual day-trip to Blackpool	One week annual holiday in Blackpool, school trips, tumble tots class, cub scouts, scout trips and camp
Swimming 40 times a year, walking, cycling	Swimming 51 times a year, walking, cycling, football match
Cinema twice a year plus any free activities organised locally	Cinema 3 times a year, panto, ice show, Tower of London, British Museum, Bradford Photo Museum, Bird Sanctuary

The slightly higher cost of household goods in the low cost budget is largely attributable to using the differential method to estimate the child budget component in the low cost budget. For example, furniture in the communal area is not identified as cost of the child in the modest-but-adequate budget, although a small percentage of the costs of replacement owing to a higher wear and tear rate in families with children is included. In the low cost child budget, the child shares the extra furnishing costs. This is because the house is much bigger for the family with children (three bedroomed terrace house) than the family without children (one bedroomed flat) and therefore requires a higher cost for overall household furnishing.

In terms of the housing, food and clothing components, the low cost child budget is between 56% and 83% of the modest-but-adequate standard. However, for the less essential components such as transport and leisure services the difference is more marked: the low cost transport budget is only 5% of the modest-but-adequate budget, mainly owing to car ownership in the latter standard, and the low cost leisure services budget is 19% of the corresponding modest-but-adequate budget.

TABLE 20: **A comparison of the low cost budget and the modest-but-adequate budget for a child aged under 11, April 1993 prices, £ per week and percentage**

	Low cost (LC) £	Modest-but-adequate (MbA) £	LC/MbA (%)
Housing	5.14	6.16	83
Fuel	3.84	2.40	160
Food	10.21	12.84	79
Clothing	4.12	7.32	56
Household goods	3.95	3.70	107
Household services	0.00	0.14	0
Personal care	0.45	1.04	44
Transport (total):	(0.27)	(4.99)	(5)
Motoring	0.00	2.50	0
Fares and other costs	0.27	2.49	11
Leisure goods	1.77	3.74	47
Leisure services	0.61	3.14	19
Child care:			
Day care	0.00	12.29	0
Baby-sitting	0.00	1.33	0
Total	30.37	59.10	51
Total less housing	25.23	52.94	48
Total plus child care costs	**43.99**	**59.10**	**74**

The low cost budget is around half the modest-but-adequate budget. This ratio is similar to the relationship between the 'prevailing family standard' and 'social minimum standard' as defined by Watts.[1] According to Watts the prevailing family standard 'affords full opportunity to participate in contemporary society and the basic options it offers. It is moderate in the sense of lying both well above the requirements of survival and decency, and well below levels of luxury as generally understood.' The social minimum standard 'lies in a boundary zone below which social concern has been traditionally and properly directed to potential issues of deficiency and deprivation.' It is set at half the prevailing family standard.

EQUIVALENCE SCALES

One of the purposes of the budget standards approach is to derive what are called 'equivalence scales'. These are used to adjust income to take account of different family sizes. This reflects the extent to which families require different incomes to achieve the same standard of living. The scales give different weights to adults and children of different ages. The advantage of the budget standards method is that equivalence scales can be derived independently of expenditure data (which is the usual way they are derived).

Table 21 compares a number of child equivalence scales. The scales are assumed to be for families with two children. For a child aged under 11, the low cost child scale after housing is higher than modest-but-adequate child scales, McClements (widely used in government statistics), younger children in Piachaud's scales and the implied equivalence scales in the income support rates, but it is the same as the implied scale in income support rates if family premium is included as well as the OECD scale. In the case of modest-but-adequate budget scales, the weight given to the child aged 4 is slightly higher than that to the child aged 10 because of the higher child care costs required for the younger child.

Child equivalence scales for low income families tend to be higher than they are at higher incomes. Thus, the equivalence scales derived from the low cost budget can be compared with those implied by the income support scales and by Piachaud for his estimate of the costs of a child. The child equivalence scales derived from the modest-but-adequate scales can be compared with the OECD and McClements scales. The low cost budget indicates that a couple with two children aged under 11 need 1.58 times the income of a childless couple. This is identical to the implied scale in income support rates but more than the Piachaud scale which suggests a ratio of

1.50. These ratios are lower at the modest–but–adequate income level – the couple with two children need 1.43 times the income of the couple to achieve the same living standards. This compares with 1.41 for the McClements scale. Given this range of equivalence ratios, it is clearly important when employing them to have regard to the level of living that they are being used to represent.

TABLE 21: **Comparison of equivalence scales, by age of the child**

	Age	Before housing	After housing
Couple family = 1.00			
Low cost budget	0-10	0.26	0.29
Modest-but-adequate budget	4	0.26	0.22
	10	0.24	0.21
	16	0.27	0.24
Income support 1993/94	0-10		0.22
	11-15		0.32
	16-17		0.38
Income support plus family premium 1993/94	0-10		0.29
	11-15		0.39
	16-17		0.45
OECD			0.29
McClements	2-4		0.18
	5-7		0.21
	8-10		0.23
	11-12		0.26
	13-15		0.28
	16-18		0.38
Piachaud	2		0.23
	5		0.27
	8		0.32
	11		0.35

Source: North Yorkshire Welfare Benefits Service 1993; P Townsend, *Meaningful Statistics on Poverty*, 1991, p15; P Whiteford, *A Family's Needs: Equivalence Scales, Poverty and Social Security*, 1985, pp108-11

NOTES

1   H Watts, *New American Budget Standards*, Institute for Research on Poverty, University of Wisconsin, 1980, pviii

7 A comparison of modest-but-adequate budgets and foster care boarding out allowances

When local authorities place children with foster parents, they pay the foster care boarding out allowance. According to the 1988 Boarding Out Allowance Regulation[1] such allowances would be sufficient 'to care for the child placed with the foster parent *as if he were a member of the foster parent's family*' (our emphasis).

TABLE 22: **Comparison of the North Yorkshire boarding out allowance and the FBU cost of a child estimates,* April 1993 prices, £ per week**

Age of child	Sibling numbers	Modest-but-adequate boy's costs	Basic boarding out foster care allowance	Shortfall/gain	Shortfall/gain as a % of foster care allowance
4	2	43.03	43.98	0.95	2%
10	2	52.63	53.75	1.12	2%
16	2	66.09	88.03	21.94	25%
4	1	51.53	43.98	−7.55	17%
10	1	61.13	53.76	−7.37	14%
16	1	73.26	88.03	14.77	17%

* Excluding child care costs but including owner occupied housing costs

Table 22 compares the FBU-derived child costs with the North Yorkshire boarding out allowances. Child care costs have not been included in the calculation since the amount that foster parents should receive for their child care services is the subject of future research. The results indicate that the North Yorkshire age-related boarding out allowance is adequate to meet the day to day costs of caring for children aged 4 and 10 years, and is more than adequate to meet the costs of a 16-year-old child.[2] However, this is assuming that the foster child shares the joint consumption costs of the placement family, such as housing, household durables, baby-sitting, family games and motoring costs. To treat the foster child as an only child, the boarding out allowance would need to be increased by 14-17% for the younger children, although it is still adequate for the 16-year-old child.

METHODS

The assumptions made about the lifestyle and circumstances of foster families on which the budget standard for the two parent family have been founded are compared in Table 23. Bebbington and Miles[3] found that 30% of the sample of 2,694 foster parents in 13 LAs in England in 1987 fitted the archetypal foster family description. The assumptions made in our profiles of two parent families with children and those characteristics found in foster families identified by Bebbington and Miles appear to describe similar, though not identical, lifestyles and living conditions. Despite this the FBU-derived cost of a child at a modest-but-adequate standard of living represents an appropriate measure of the cost of a natural child in a foster family environment.

However, two further problems remain:

- Should the child in the foster family be paid expenses by the LA as an only child or as a child in a two child family?
- What is a standard measure of foster care allowance, given that the authorities in England determine their own boarding out allowances?

The model used to estimate the cost of a natural child living in a family results in different costs according to the age of the child and the family size. That is, the greater the number of children the lower the cost of the child estimate in certain major component parts of the budget standard. The question really addresses the issue of whether a foster child should be maintained by the local authority as an individual divorced from the existing joint consumption, or as sharing the joint consumption of the placement family.

TABLE 23: **Comparison of lifestyles of the FBU two parent family and the typical foster family**

Modest-but-adequate	Foster family
3 bed LA or O/O dwelling	3 or more bedrooms
1 parent full-time work 1 parent part-time work **Income** middle income range	1 parent full-time work 1 part-time or not at all **Occupation** Skilled man./own account 29% Intermed. non-manual 18% semi skill./personal service 16% employer/manager 10%
Two parent family	7 out of 8 are two parent families
Male aged 34/37, female aged 32/35 years	Female aged 31-55 years
Motor vehicle ownership (5 years old)	
Dependent own children age 4 age 10 age 16	Dependent own children 5+ Average age, youngest child 10 one child 21% } two child 25% } 46% none 37%
FBU Family Two parent, one in full-time and one in part-time work, two children 4 years+, 3 bed house	**Archetypal foster family** Two parent, one in full-time employment, dependent children 5+, 3 (or more) bed house

Source of foster family data: Bebbington and Miles (1989)

The boarding out allowance is paid to all foster parents regardless of other enhancements, and special payments are made in some cases. The North Yorkshire foster care rates shown above are selected as an example of a middle range of the rates paid by local authorities in England. The city of York is also the geographical centre for pricing the FBU budget. The basic boarding out annual allowance includes an extra week's allowance for one week's holiday, the foster child's birthday, and additional expenses for Christmas week. The allowance shown below is based on 55 allowances per year, and the sum is intended to cover all the normal expenses, including certain clothing renewal costs in respect of caring for the child. In addition the foster parent can claim an initial clothing grant for new foster children of up to five boarding out allowance payments over the period of the first year, and an extra two weeks' holiday money if the foster family goes away from home on holiday for three weeks each year.

NOTES

1   CM 2184, 1988, p15
2   No account has been taken in this analysis for the extra costs of foster care – ie, the costs over and above those of a natural child in her/his own family. The additional or special costs of foster caring are also the subject of future research being undertaken by Oldfield (forthcoming).
3   A Bebbington and J Miles, *The Supply of Foster Families for Children in Care*, PSSRU Discussion Paper 624/4, University of Kent, 1989

8 A comparison of the low cost budget and benefit rates

The low cost family budgets indicate that a couple with two children under 11 need £180.30 a week to maintain a low cost standard of living, while the lone mother with two children needs £145.83 in April 1993. If maximum housing benefit and council tax benefit are taken into account, the budgets are £142.56 and £111.73 for the 2 adult/2 child and lone parent/2 child families respectively.

Income support is a safety-net providing a minimum amount for people to live on if they are on a low or no income and have limited capital. Parents eligible for income support with two children aged under 11 currently receive £108.75 a week of which £39.75 represents child allowance for the two children. A single parent with two children receives £88.65 including £44.65 child allowance to feed and clothe their children and keep them warm, clean and healthy.

Although the low cost budgets are fairly stringent, income support rates do not allow the families with children to reach even a low cost standard of living.

TABLE 24: **Comparison of the low cost budgets and the income support rate for 2 adult/2 child and 1 adult/2 child families, April 1993 prices, £ per week**

	Low cost budget	Income support	Shortfall
2 adult/2 child	142.56	108.75	33.81
1 adult/2 child	111.73	88.65	23.08

Table 24 compares the low cost budgets and income support rates for families with children. The low cost budgets are about 30% higher than the 1993/94 income support rates. Although rent and council tax are both assumed to be fully covered by benefits, the couple with two children aged under 11 nevertheless require a supplement of £34 per week in addition to income support to achieve the low cost standard. This supplementary figure is £23 per week for a lone parent with two children.

The low cost budget for a child is based on the average cost of a child in the 2 adult/2 child family and is £30.37 per child per week. If full housing benefits and council tax benefits are taken into account, the low cost budget for a child (aged under 11) less rent is estimated to be £25.62 per week at April 1993 prices.

Table 25 compares the income support rates, family premium and child benefit with the low cost budget for a child aged under 11 in April 1993. Child benefit covers 39% of the cost of a child in a one child family and 35% for the child in a two child family. The income support scales for children are also inadequate to meet the low cost standard, only covering 59% of the low cost budget for a child. An extra £10 in addition to the income support child scale is required if the low cost standard is to be met.

TABLE 25: **A comparison of income support rates, family premium and child benefit with low cost budgets for a child aged under 11, April 1993 prices**

		1 child family	(%)*	2 child family	(%)*
Child benefit,	first child	£10.00	39	£10.00	39
	second child			£8.10	32
	average (2 children)			£ 9.05	35
Income support (aged 0-10)		£15.05	59	£15.05	59
Income support + family premium		£24.70	96	£19.88	78
Low cost budget (LC)		£28.69	–	£25.62	100
Shortfall for a child in:		1 child family		2 child family	
Child benefit		£18.69		£16.57	
Income support		£13.64		£10.57	
Income support + family premium		£3.99		£ 5.74	

*Percentages show the benefit rates expressed as a percentage of the low cost child budget in a 2 child family.

If the family premium is treated as part of the income support scales for children then the extent to which the low cost of a child is met depends on the number of children in a family. There is still a discrepancy in a two child family of £5.74. For a one child family the discrepancy is more difficult to estimate because the low cost budget was not calculated for a one child family and therefore did not take account of (dis)economies of scale. Based on the estimates of economies of scale derived from the modest-but-adequate budget we estimate that a single child would need £28.69 on the low cost budget which is still £3.99 short of the income support scales for a child if the family premium is counted as support for that child.

9 Conclusion

This chapter draws together the main findings of this study and highlights their implications in the context of current benefit rates and child care provisions.

This study is the most elaborate attempt since Piachaud in 1979 to estimate the direct cost of a child. It shows the costs of a child at two levels – modest-but-adequate and low cost. At a modest-but-adequate living standard, the cost of a child excluding child care increases with age, boys cost more than girls, and the cost of an only child in local authority tenure depending on age is between £6.11 and £7.44 more than a child in a two child family, at April 1993 prices. A child aged under 11 in a two adult two child family living in a local authority dwelling costs £59.10 per week at a modest-but-adequate level. The low cost budget, though cheaper than the modest-but-adequate and fairly stringent, still costs £30.37 a week – including £10.21 to feed the child, £4.12 for clothes, £3.84 to keep the child warm, and £2.38 for entertainment, toys and leisure.

Child care costs are not included in the low cost budget, the assumption being that at least one parent (or the lone parent) does not work at all but tends to the child's needs full-time. Nevertheless the modest-but-adequate budget has shown that, if the mother is in employment, child care costs for a pre-school child constitutes a major proportion of the overall budget of families. The cheapest formal childminding arrangements for the two children for both parents or the lone parent working full-time is £60.79 per week (assuming the child aged 4 years attends a pre-school class for part of the day). In the case of one of the parents or the lone parent working part-time, the cost is £24.59. This suggests that for lone parents with young children on income support, such child care costs create a poverty trap and act as a disincentive to seek out employment. Affordable child care costs could encourage parents with children of pre-school age to take part in the labour market, and so, in the case of lone parents in poverty, reduce their reliance on welfare benefits. The UK currently has the second lowest level of subsidised child care in the European Community. Improving state child care provision would lessen the present wastage of both financial and human assets.

Our findings also show that income support – the safety net which provides the minimum amount of income for people to live on – is far from a modest-but-adequate standard and does not allow the families with children to reach even a low cost standard of living. Income support including the family premium meets only 78% of the low cost budget of a child in a two adult two child family, while income support child allowance meets only 59% and child benefit meets only 35%. Such a family would require a supplement of £5.74 per week in addition to income support child rate plus family premium to achieve the low cost child standard.

Measuring the costs of a child is of practical importance in policy relating to the welfare level of families with children. When the results of the Family Budget Unit budget standard research were launched, the following exchanges took place in the House of Commons:

'I hope that the Secretary of State has noted and studied the Rowntree Report, by Professor Jonathan Bradshaw, which was published earlier this week. The report underlined the difficulties of making ends meet at current income support levels. Does the Right Hon. Gentleman accept that there is little room for comfort when – according to the report's findings – a couple with two children under 11, living in a council house, need an extra £36 per week to fund the austere low cost budget? There are no signs that this Minister and this Government have any visible or active commitment to tackling the problems of poverty.'
Mr Donald Dewar (Labour Spokesman on Social Security)

'The Hon. Gentlemen said that the Rowntree report spelt out an "austere low cost budget" – a budget that allows the poorest only a video recorder, a camera, and a television set...'
Mr Peter Lilley (Secretary of State for Social Security)

Hansard, 12 November 1992, cols 1018 and 1020

In our judgement, the low cost budget in this study is a restricted one, but Mr Lilley's comments can be taken as a useful starting point. Ignoring for the moment the effect on quality of life, removing the video recorder, camera, radio/cassette recorder and television set from the low cost budget for a 2 adult/2 child family would reduce the overall cost of the budget by £4.31 per week (April 1993 prices). This saving could be increased to £5.63 if Mr Lilley took the view that families on income support should not be able to afford a day trip to Blackpool once per year.

However, this saving would be spread across the whole family – the child's share would be only £0.66 – hardly enough to meet the shortfall of the current child scale rates of income support! To do that, Mr Lilley would need to find as much as a further £5.08 in savings from this low cost budget for a child. What further items mentioned in the low cost budget should the 2.7 million children dependent on income support do without?

In the meantime, policies already being implemented are likely to stretch the current income support rates even further. This study gives an indication to the likely effect of VAT on fuel for families on low incomes. At a modest-but-adequate budget level, the proportion of child costs, less housing, spent on fuel is 5%. This percentage increases to 15% for the low cost child budget. This is not just because the low cost budget itself is smaller, and fuel is a fixed cost – although this has a significant part to play. Families on low incomes actually spend more money on fuel than similar families on average income levels, largely because of a combination of poorer insulation due to lower quality housing and the need to heat the dwelling for more hours each day. This second factor is particularly strong in the case of families with children. As a result, families on low incomes with children will be of necessity worse hit by taxation on fuel than even families on a higher incomes, and ensuring that, unless income support levels are altered to adequately reflect this increase in essential costs, the already significant shortfall between income support rates and the low cost budget will become even greater.

MODEST-BUT-ADEQUATE CLOTHING

An example of the full clothing budgets for a boy aged 10 years is shown below:

Item	description	outlet	price-£	no	life (yrs)	total cost	cost/yr	cost/wk
Main items								
jacket	winter	C&A	24.99	1	2	24.99	12.50	0.240
jacket	waterproof	Milletts	13.99	1	3	13.99	4.66	0.090
tracksuit top		C&A	6.99	1	2	6.99	3.50	0.067
tracksuit bottoms		C&A	7.99	2	1	15.98	15.98	0.307
school trousers		BHS	9.99	2	1	19.98	19.98	0.384
jeans	denim	C&A	9.99	2	1	19.98	19.98	0.384
trousers	casual	C&A	12.99	1	1	12.99	12.99	0.250
trousers	smart	C&A	12.99	1	1	12.99	12.99	0.250
school shirt	long-sl	BHS	7.99	2	2	15.98	7.99	0.154
shirt	casual	C&A	7.99	3	2	23.97	11.99	0.230
school jumper		BHS	8.99	2	1	17.98	17.98	0.346
jumper	winter	BHS	9.99	3	2	29.97	14.99	0.288
sweatshirt	long-sl	C&A	6.99	2	2	13.98	6.99	0.134
jacket	summer	BHS	19.99	1	2	19.99	10.00	0.192
school shirt	short-sl	C&A	3.99	2	2	7.98	3.99	0.077
shirt	short-sl	C&A	5.99	2	2	11.98	5.99	0.115
t-shirt	short-sl	BHS	7.99	2	2	15.98	7.99	0.154
t-shirt	plain	BHS	5.99	2	2	11.98	5.99	0.115
t-shirt	cartoon	BHS	6.99	2	2	13.98	6.99	0.134
jumper	summer	BHS	9.99	1	2	9.99	5.00	0.096
shorts	casual	C&A	4.99	1	2	4.99	2.50	0.048
PE shirt		BHS	6.99	2	2	13.98	6.99	0.134
PE shorts		Olympus	3.99	1	2	3.99	2.00	0.038
neckerchief	scout-cub	scout shop	2.00	1	5	2.00	0.40	0.008
garter tabs	scout-cub	scout shop	0.69	1	5	0.69	0.14	0.003
shorts	scout-cub	scout shop	8.70	1	2	8.70	4.35	0.084

Item	description	outlet	price-£	no	life (yrs)	total cost	cost/yr	cost/wk
sweatshirt	scout-cub	scout shop	5.75	1	3	5.75	1.92	0.037
socks	scout-cub	scout shop	1.99	2	2	3.98	1.99	0.038
swimming trunks		C&A	3.99	1	2	3.99	2.00	0.038
underpants	pack 5	BHS	5.99	3	2	17.97	8.99	0.173
pyjamas		BHS	8.99	2	2	17.98	8.99	0.173
dressing gown		BHS	14.99	1	2	14.99	7.50	0.144
socks	winter-3pk	BHS	3.99	3	1	11.97	11.97	0.230
socks	summer-3pk	BHS	3.50	2	1	7.00	7.00	0.135
socks	football	Olympus	1.99	2	2	3.98	1.99	0.038
sub-total						**443.61**	**277.20**	**5.328**
Accessories								
hat	winter peak cap	C&A	4.50	1	2	4.50	2.25	0.043
hat	baseball peak cap	C&A	2.99	1	2	2.99	1.50	0.029
scarf	knitted	Milletts	3.99	1	2	3.99	2.00	0.038
gloves	football padded	Argos	4.99	1	2	4.99	2.50	0.048
sub-total						**16.47**	**8.25**	**0.158**
Footwear								
shoes	'Doc Martens' heavy duty	Saxone	24.99	1	1	24.99	24.99	0.481
shoes	school, smart lace-up	Saxone	18.99	3	1	56.97	56.97	1.096
trainers	'Hi Tec' lace-up	Saxone	17.99	2	1	35.98	35.98	0.692
pumps	casual, lace-up	Saxone	4.99	1	1	4.99	4.99	0.096
PE	lace up	Saxone	4.99	2	1	9.98	9.98	0.192
slippers	cartoon	Saxone	6.99	1	1	6.99	6.99	0.134
sub-total						**139.90**	**139.90**	**2.691**

MODEST-BUT-ADEQUATE TOYS AND HOBBIES

Item	outlet	price	qty	life/yr	cost/yr	cost/wk	£ wk aged 4	£ wk aged 10	£ wk aged 16
games compendium	W H Smith	9.99	1	10	1.00	0.019	0.010	0.010	0.010
domino set	W H Smith	2.50	1	10	0.25	0.005	0.003	0.003	0.003
rally car	Argos	12.50	1	4	3.13	0.060	0.000	0.060	0.000
lego motor set	Argos	18.00	1	4	4.50	0.087	0.000	0.087	0.000
LCD games	Argos	12.99	1	3	4.33	0.083	0.000	0.083	0.000
LCD games	Argos	16.49	1	3	5.50	0.106	0.000	0.106	0.000
jigsaw	W H Smith	4.45	1	3	1.48	0.029	0.000	0.029	0.000
pass the pigs	W H Smith	5.09	1	5	1.02	0.020	0.000	0.020	0.000
cluedo	W H Smith	8.75	1	5	1.75	0.034	0.000	0.034	0.000
model aircraft kit	Argos	12.99	1	2	6.50	0.125	0.000	0.125	0.000
paint/colour kit	Argos	15.49	1	1	15.49	0.298	0.000	0.298	0.000
chemistry set	Argos	14.25	1	3	4.75	0.091	0.000	0.091	0.000
skate board	Argos	14.99	1	3	5.00	0.096	0.000	0.096	0.000
knee/shin pads	Argos	8.99	1	3	3.00	0.058	0.000	0.058	0.000
swing ball	Argos	12.99	1	5	2.60	0.050	0.000	0.050	0.000
bicycle helmet	Argos	15.99	1	4	4.00	0.077	0.000	0.077	0.000
bicycle	Halford	149.99	1	4	37.50	0.721	0.000	0.721	0.000
inner tube	Halford	3.69	1	4	0.92	0.018	0.000	0.018	0.000
puncture repair kit	Halford	2.69	1	1	2.69	0.052	0.000	0.052	0.000
doll	Argos	15.75	1	4	3.94	0.076	0.076	0.000	0.000
doll's buggy	Argos	20.50	1	4	5.13	0.099	0.099	0.000	0.000
doll	Argos	9.89	1	3	3.30	0.063	0.063	0.000	0.000
play dough set	Argos	7.49	1	2	3.75	0.072	0.072	0.000	0.000
child's scissors	E L Centre	1.65	1	2	0.83	0.016	0.016	0.000	0.000
paint set	W H Smith	4.59	1	1	4.59	0.088	0.088	0.000	0.000

Item	outlet	price	qty	life/yr	cost/yr	cost/wk	£ wk aged 4	£ wk aged 10	£ wk aged 16
plasticine	W H Smith	0.85	1	1	0.85	0.016	0.016	0.000	0.000
child's glue	E L Centre	1.75	2	1	3.50	0.067	0.067	0.000	0.000
glue brush	E L Centre	0.42	1	1	0.42	0.008	0.008	0.000	0.000
paint brush	E L Centre	0.59	2	2	0.59	0.011	0.011	0.000	0.000
paint brush	E L Centre	0.85	2	2	0.85	0.016	0.016	0.000	0.000
gummed squares	W H Smith	0.85	1	1	10.85	0.016	0.016	0.000	0.000
thick chalks	E L Centre	0.85	1	1	0.85	0.016	0.016	0.000	0.000
wax crayons	E L Centre	0.85	1	1	0.85	0.016	0.016	0.000	0.000
coloured paper	W H Smith	4.09	2	1	8.18	0.157	0.157	0.000	0.000
coloured paper book	E L Centre	0.99	2	1	1.98	0.038	0.038	0.000	0.000
wipe/chalk board	E L Centre	4.25	3	2	6.38	0.123	0.123	0.000	0.000
colour playcloth & crayons	E L Centre	1.99	1	2	1.00	0.019	0.019	0.000	0.000
magic paintbook	W H Smith	1.99	4	1	7.96	0.153	0.153	0.000	0.000
fuzzy felt	E L Centre	2.99	2	3	1.99	0.038	0.038	0.000	0.000
number jigsaw	E L Centre	3.24	1	2	1.63	0.031	0.031	0.000	0.000
jigsaw puzzle	E L Centre	4.25	3	2	6.38	0.123	0.123	0.000	0.000
picture pairs	E L Centre	2.99	1	3	2.99	1.00	0.019	0.019	0.000
snap	E L Centre	0.99	1	3	0.33	0.006	0.006	0.000	0.000
buckeroo	Argos	7.50	1	3	2.50	0.048	0.048	0.000	0.000
blow bubbles	W H Smith	1.00	2	1	2.00	0.038	0.038	0.000	0.000
glove puppet	Argos	5.99	1	3	2.00	0.038	0.038	0.000	0.000
wooden bead set	W H Smith	3.99	1	2	2.00	0.038	0.038	0.000	0.000
farm yard set	Argos	4.99	1	3	1.66	0.032	0.032	0.000	0.000
soft toy	Argos	4.99	1	4	1.25	0.024	0.024	0.000	0.000
play house	Argos	13.49	1	2	6.75	0.130	0.130	0.000	0.000
lego set	Argos	22.00	1	5	4.40	0.085	0.085	0.000	0.000
bucket sand set	E L Centre	3.25	1	2	1.63	0.031	0.031	0.000	0.000
paddling pool	E L Centre	5.99	1	3	2.00	0.038	0.038	0.000	0.000
soft football	E L Centre	2.99	1	2	1.50	0.029	0.029	0.000	0.000

Item	outlet	price	qty	life/yr	cost/yr	cost/wk	£ wk aged 4	£ wk aged 10	£ wk aged 16
tricycle and sandbox	Argos	24.99	1	3	8.33	0.160	0.160	0.000	0.000
single swing	E L Centre	21.95	1	6	3.66	0.070	0.070	0.000	0.000
paint/colour kit	Argos	15.49	1	2	7.75	0.149	0.000	0.000	0.149
jewellery kit	Argos	10.99	1	2	5.50	0.105	0.000	0.000	0.105
sub-total							**2.061**	**2.037**	**0.267**

LOW COST CLOTHING

Girl's clothing (aged 4 years) October 1991 prices

Item	description	retailer	price £	number	life (yrs)	cost/wk £
Outerwear						
winter coat	zipped front, elasticated cuffs, cotton	BHS*	14.99	1	2	0.14
winter dress	knitted style, acrylic	C&A	6.99	1	1	0.13
winter dress	long sleeves, acrylic	C&A**	6.99	1	1	0.13
winter trousers	elasticated waist, cotton	C&A	5.99	1	0.75	0.15
winter skirt	elasticated waist, cotton	BHS**	4.99	1	1.5	0.06
blouse	long sleeves, polyester/cotton	BHS	6.99	1	0.75	0.18
winter cardigan/ sweater	long sleeves, acrylic	C&A	4.99	3	1.5	0.19
summer dress	cap sleeves, T-shirt style, cotton/polyester	C&A	4.99	2	1	0.04
summer skirt	elasticated waist, cotton	BHS	6.99	1	1.5	0.09
summer trousers	elasticated waist, cotton	C&A	7.99	1	0.75	0.21
shorts	elasticated waist, cotton	BHS	6.99	1	1.5	0.09
blouse	short sleeves, cotton	C&A	7.99	1	0.75	0.21
T-shirt	short sleeves, cotton	BHS	3.99	2	0.75	0.21
swimsuit	all-in-one, nylon	C&A	5.99	1	1.5	0.08
Underwear/Nightwear						
pants, pk of 5	assorted briefs, cotton	BHS	4.99	2	0.8	0.24
vests, pk of 2	sleeveless, cotton	BHS	4.99	2	1.4	0.14
night shirt, winter	long sleeves, cotton	BHS	7.99	2	1.5	0.21
night shirt, summer	s-sleeves, short length, polyester	BHS	8.99	2	1.5	0.23
dressing gown	l-sleeves, polyester	BHS	10.99	1	2	0.11
thick tights	ribbed, acrylic	C&A	1.75	2	1.5	0.05
ankle socks, pk of 5	cotton	BHS	5.50	2	0.8	0.26
Accessories						
gloves	knitted style, acrylic	C&A	1.99	1	2	0.02

Item	description	retailer	price £	number	life (yrs)	cost/wk £
Footwear						
smart shoes	buckle fastened, leather uppers	Saxone	11.99	2	1	0.46
pumps	canvas	Saxone	4.99	1	0.5	0.19
slippers	fur-lined	BHS	4.99	1	0.5	0.19
Total weekly cost – £						**4.01**

* cheapest prices ** sales prices

Boy's clothing (aged 10 years) October 1991 prices

Item	description	retailer	price £	number	life (yrs)	cost/wk £
Outerwear						
water-proof jacket	zipped front, hood, elasticated hem, nylon	Millets Astral	13.99	1	2.00	0.14
jeans	fitted waist, denim	C&A	9.99	1	0.75	0.26
casual trousers	fitted waist, cotton/polyester	C&A	12.99	1	0.75	0.33
smart trousers	pleats, belt, polyester/viscose	C&A	12.99	1	0.75	0.33
casual shirt	long sleeves, collar,cotton	C&A	5.99	3	0.75	0.46
winter jumper	long sleeves, crew neck,acrylic	BHS	9.99	2	1.50	0.26
sweatshirt	long sleeves, crew neck, polyester/cotton	C&A	6.99	1	1.50	0.09
T-shirt, plain	short sleeves, cotton	BHS**	3.99	2	1.50	0.10
vest T-shirt	short sleeves, cotton	BHS	3.99	2	0.75	0.21
casual shorts	elasticated waist, cotton	C&A	4.99	1	1.50	0.06
swimming trunks	elastic/ drawstring waist, nylon/elastine	C&A	3.99	1	1.50	0.05
Underwear/Nightwear						
underpants, pk of 5	brief slips, cotton	BHS	5.99	1	0.63	0.18
winter pyjamas	tracksuit style, cotton	BHS	8.99	1	1.00	0.17
summer pyjamas	traditional style, cotton/polyester	BHS	8.99	1	1.00	0.17
dressing gown	wrap-over, cotton	BHS	14.99	1	2.00	0.14
winter socks, pk of 3	medium length, cotton/nylon	BHS	3.99	3	1.00	0.23
summer socks, pk of 5	short length, cotton/nylon	BHS	5.50	2	1.00	0.21

Item	description	retailer	price £	number	life (yrs)	cost/wk £
Accessories						
gloves	knitted style, acrylic	C&A	1.99	1	2.00	0.02
Footwear						
school/smart shoes	plain upper, lace-up	Saxone	18.99	2	1.00	0.73
casual pumps	canvas	Saxone	4.99	1	0.50	0.19
slippers	slip-on, cartoon	Saxone	6.99	1	1.00	0.13
Total weekly cost – £						**4.46**

* cheapest prices ** sales prices

BIBLIOGRAPHY

Anderson, B R, Clark, A J, Baldwin, R and Milbank, N O (1985) *Building Research Establishment Domestic Energy Model: Background, Philosophy and Description,* Building Research Establishment Publications.

Banks, J and Johnson, P (1993) *Children and Household Living Standards,* London, The Institute For Fiscal Studies.

Bebbington, A and Miles, J (1989) *The Supply of Foster Families for Children in Care,* PSSRU Discussion Paper 624/4, University of Kent, PSSRU.

Birds Eye Wall's Ltd (1991) *Wall's Pocket Money Monitor,* Bird's Eye Walls Ltd, Surrey.

Borgeraas, E (1987) *Et Standardbudsjett for Forbruksutgifter,* Lysaker, Statens Institutt for Forbruksforskning.

Bradshaw, J (1993) *Household Budgets and Living Standards,* A Joseph Rowntree Report.

Bradshaw, J (1993) *Budget Standards for the United Kingdom,* Aldershot, Avebury (forthcoming).

Bradshaw, J (1988) 'Welfare benefits' in *Money Matters, Income, Wealth and Financial Welfare,* eds Walker, R and Parker, G, London, Sage Publications Ltd.

Bradshaw, J, Mitchell, D and Morgan, J (1987) 'Evaluating Adequacy: the potential of budget standards', *Journal of Social Policy,* 16:2, pp 165-181.

Bradshaw, J and Morgan, J (1987) *Budgeting on Benefit: The consumption of families on social security,* Occasional Paper 5, London, Family Policy Studies Centre.

Bradshaw, J and Holmes, H (1989) *Living on the Edge: A Study of the Living Standards of Families on Benefit in Tyne and Wear,* London, Child Poverty Action Group Ltd.

Bradshaw, J and Ernst, J (1990) *Establishing a Modest-But-Adequate Budget for a British Family,* Working Paper No 2, Family Budget Unit, University of York.

Bradshaw, J (1991) *Seeking a Behavioural Representation of Modest-But-Adequate Levels of Living,* Working Paper No 13, Family Budget Unit, University of York.

Bradshaw, J, Hicks, L and Parker, H (1992) *Summary Budget Standards for Six Households,* Working Paper No 12 (Revised), Family Budget Unit, University of York.

Central Statistical Office (1990) *Family Expenditure Survey 1988,* London, HMSO.

Cohen, B (1988) *Caring For Children, Services and Policies for Childcare and Equal Opportunities in the UK*, London, Family Policy Studies Centre.

Cm 2184 (1988) *Boarding Out Allowance Regulation*, London, HMSO.

Conniffe, D and Keogh, G (1988) *Equivalence Scales and Costs of Children*, Paper No 142, Dublin, The Economic and Social Research Institute.

Department of Employment (1993) *Employment Gazette*, London, HMSO June 1993.

Department of Transport (1988) *National Travel Survey: 1985-6 Report – Part One, An Analysis of Personal Travel*, London, HMSO.

Department of Transport (1989) *Transport Statistics Great Britain 1978-88*, London, HMSO.

Department of Transport (1991) *Transport Statistics Great Britain 1991*, London, HMSO.

Field, F (1985) *What Price a Child? A historical review of the relative cost of dependants*, Studies of the Social Security System No 8, London, Policy Studies Institute.

Frayman, H (1991) *Breadline Britain 1990s*, London, Domino Films/London Weekend Television.

Furnham, A and Lewis, A (1986) *Economic Mind: The Social Psychology of Economic Behaviour*, Brighton, Wheatsheaf Books.

Henley Centre (1991) 'Time Budgets', *Leisure Futures*, November 1991, pp21-35.

Hicks, L and Ernst, J (1992) *Modest-But-Adequate Budget Standards, Housing Budgets for Six Household Types*, Working Paper No 5, Family Budget Unit, University of York.

Hicks, L and Ernst, J (1992) *Modest-But-Adequate Budget Standards, Transport Budgets for Six Household Types*, Working Paper No 6, Family Budget Unit, University of York.

Hutton, S and Wilkinson, B (1992) *Modest-But-Adequate Budget Standards, Fuel Budgets for Six Household Types*, Working Paper No 8, Family Budget Unit, University of York.

Hill, M (1992) 'Children's roles in the domestic economy', *Journal of Consumer Studies and Home Economics* 16, pp33-50.

Joshi, H (1987) *The Cash Opportunity Costs of Childbearing: An Approach to Estimation using British Data*, Centre for Economic Policy Research, Paper 208.

Lovering, K (1984) *Cost of Children in Australia*, Working Paper 8, Australian Institute of Family Studies.

McCabe, M and Kirk, D (1992) *Modest-But-Adequate Budget Standards, Household Goods and Services Budgets for Six Household Types,* Working Paper No 10, Family Budget Unit, University of York.

McCabe, M and Rose, A (1992) *Modest-But-Adequate Budget Standards, Clothing Budgets for Six Household Types,* Working Paper No 9, Family Budget Unit, University of York.

McCabe, M and Waddington, A (1992) *Modest-But-Adequate Budget Standards, Leisure Budgets for Six Household Types,* Working Paper No 11, Family Budget Unit, University of York.

McClements, L D (1978) *The Economics of Social Security,* London, Heinemann.

McClements, L D (1977) *Equivalence Scales for Children,* Journal of Public Economics, Vol 8, No 2, pp191-210.

Millar, J (1989) *Poverty and the Lone-parent Family,* London, Avebury: Gower.

Ministry of Agriculture Fisheries and Food (1985-1989) *Household Food Consumption and Expenditure (National Food Survey) 1983-87,* London, HMSO.

National Advisory Committee on Nutritional Education (NACNE) (1983) *Proposals and Guidelines for Health Education in Britain,* London, Health Education Council.

Nelson, M (1986) 'The distribution of nutrient intake within families', *British Journal of Nutrition* 55, pp267-277.

Nelson, M , Mayer, A B , and Manley, P (1992) *Modest-But-Adequate Budget Standards, Food Budgets for Six Household Types,* Working Paper No 4, Family Budget Unit, University of York.

North Yorkshire Welfare Benefits Service (1993) *An Adviser's Guide to Benefits 1993-4.*

Office of Population Censuses and Surveys (1991) *General Household Survey 1989,* London, HMSO.

Office of Population Censuses and Surveys (1990) *General Household Survey 1987 Supplement: Participation in Sport,* London, HMSO.

Oldfield, N (1992) *Using Budget Standards to Estimate the Cost of Children,* Working Paper No 15, Family Budget Unit, University of York.

Parker, M (1961) *Homes for Today and Tomorrow,* Ministry of Housing and Local Government, London, HMSO.

Piachaud, D (1979) *The Cost of a Child,* London, Child Poverty Action Group Ltd.

Piachaud, D (1981) *Children and Poverty,* London, Child Poverty Action Group Ltd.

Piachaud, D (1984) *Round about Fifty Hours a Week: The Time Costs of Children,* Child Poverty Action Group Ltd.

Rowntree, B S (1901) *Poverty: A Study of Town Life,* London, Macmillan.

Social Planning Council of Metropolitan Toronto (1981) *The Budgets Guide Methodology Study,* Toronto.

Social Security Committee, 2nd Report (1992) *Low Income Statistics: Low income families 1979-1989,* London, HMSO.

Social Security Select Committee (1991) *Low Income Statistics: Households below Average Income Tables 1988,* First Report 1990-91, House of Commons.

Swedish National Board for Consumer Policies (1989) *Calculations of Reasonable Costs,* Sweden.

Townsend, P (1991) *Meaningful Statistics on Poverty 1991,* No 2, Statistical Monitoring Unit, Department of Social Policy and Social Planning, University of Bristol.

Watts, H (1980) *New American Budget Standards: Report of the Expert Committee on Family Budget Revision,* University of Wisconsin, Institute for Research on Poverty.

Whiteford, P (1985) *A Family's Needs: Equivalence Scales, Poverty and Social Security,* Research Paper No 27, Development Division, Australian Department of Social Security.

Wynn, M (1972) *Family Policy: A study of the economic costs of rearing children and their social and political consequences,* London, Michael Joseph.

Yu, A C S (1992) *Modest-But-Adequate Budget Standards, Personal Care Budgets for Six Household Types,* Working Paper No 7, Family Budget Unit, University of York.

Yu, A C S (1992) *Low Cost Budget Standards for Three Household Types,* Working Paper No 17, Family Budget Unit, University of York.